Mary O'Brien M.B.E. lives in Omagh Co. Tyrone, but grew up on the family farm outside Fivemiletown where her horrific accident occurred in September 1942.

Her disability presented many challenges and obstacles but these were just something Mary had to overcome and in doing so became more resilient as the years advanced.

Mary now admits that the task her grandchildren set her – that of writing her memoir – has been one of the toughest challenges she has faced.

However, she took up her pencil, and after five years of writing and rewriting her story is now told.

Not a leg to stand on

Mary O'Brien M.B.E.

Not a leg to stand on

Vanguard Press

VANGUARD PAPERBACK

© Copyright 2013
Mary O'Brien M.B.E

A CIP catalogue record for this title is
available from the British Library.

ISBN 978-1-84386-743-2

*Vanguard Press is an imprint of
Pegasus Elliot MacKenzie Publishers Ltd.*
www.pegasuspublishers.com

First Published in 2013

**Vanguard Press
Sheraton House Castle Park
Cambridge England**

Printed & Bound in Great Britain

For my grandchildren:

Joanne, Rory, Sarah, Hannah, Jessica, Niamh and Clare

Acknowledgements

Darach MacDonald for all his hours of proofreading and Adrian Mullen who helped me find a publisher.

For their typewriting skills: Toni Mullan, Denise O'Brien and Teresa Fullan.

My own family, especially my sister Madeline and my husband John who both kept me encouraged.

All my friends in PHAB. Margaret Kane, Pat and Noreen Conway, Dorothy Griffin, Nan McCartan, Peggy Bradley (deceased), Nora Quigley, Tom Flanagan, Dr Roger Parke, Pat O'Brien, Doreen McFarland, Charlie Gilmour.

Hughie McMahon and Frankie Foy, two members of an older generation in Fivemiletown, who were a mine of information about the time of my accident.

Thank you to Dr Haldane Mitchell who inspired me to write my story.

Chapter 1

"Child loses legs"

My parents never really talked about it – the accident. If I raised the subject, Mammy would get upset. So now I can only piece together what happened from other accounts, starting with a short two-paragraph story in a local paper, "Distressing Fivemiletown Affair: Child Loses Legs". The details in the brief report are sparse and vague: an unnamed child, aged two, is entangled in a corn reaper on the farm of her father, Bernard McMahon of Breakley. With both legs severed, she is removed to Fermanagh County Hospital where she remains in a critical condition.

That's it, the sole public announcement of an event that would overshadow the rest of my life and that of my family. I cannot explain why there was no follow-up about my survival and recovery in the local press. I can only surmise now that the details were played down to save my parents from further distress. I know that they each blamed themselves for what happened, as if a single precautionary act on their part might have saved the day. But those were simpler, slower-moving times. Nobody could possibly have foreseen what happened on the morning of 26 September 1942 when I was two years old, a tiny toddler discovering the wonders and magic of life on our small family farm, nestling in the natural beauty of Tyrone's Clogher Valley.

What I do know now is this: my Uncle Johnny Keenan had the name of being a good "weather watcher" and he had predicted that the next few days would be fine and dry for the harvest. So Daddy decided to bring in the corn which had grown and ripened in a field right beside our house. He arranged with two local farm labourers, Jimmy McKeshlin and John Holden, to start the job while he looked after the routine farm work. So as Jimmy and John sharpened the blades on the corn reaper and harnessed Jimmy's own two horses, Daddy finished milking the cows, filled the churns, leaving aside a little milk for family use, and set off on the cart with his own horse Bob for the local creamery only half a mile away in Fivemiletown. Just before departing, he opened the gate to the cornfield to allow access for the men with the horse-drawn reaper.

I still have a photograph of myself from that summer, the only photo of me with my own legs. I am standing shyly with a big bunch of wildflowers picked for Mammy from the hedgerows and fields. She, meanwhile, would have been busy at her own chores, which included the housework as well as looking after the poultry and feeding the young calves and piglets. Long before most labour-saving devices, life was a hectic schedule for farm wives. Little wonder that they were occasionally distracted from what their children were up to as they roamed relatively free within the environs of the farmhouse on a warm harvest day, where the surrounding nooks and crannies provided a natural and magical playground. So the field of tall ripe corn swaying in the soft autumn breeze proved to be too much of a temptation for me and two other inquisitive youngsters – my brother John, who was three and a half years old at the time, and Hugh Hopper, a two-year-old neighbour. I was all of two years and three months and game for the adventure presented by an open gate.

Unnoticed by Mammy who was busy in the kitchen, we slipped into the field and ran off into the rows of ripened corn. Hidden beneath the swaying stalks, it was a new enchanting world for three toddlers and before too long, I lay down exhausted and fell asleep. I was soon well beyond hearing the soft clomping of the horses or the mechanical click of the reaper they drew in their wake. As John Holden commenced the mowing, he was unaware that three small children were hidden in the rows of corn stretching before him; and one was lying in the direct path of the approaching blades.

On first contact, my legs were entangled. John halted the team immediately and unhitched the reaper. But, on seeing me caught in the blades and bleeding, he was too distraught to help further, so he ran off to the house for help. Just at that, Daddy arrived home from the creamery and he rushed to the scene of horror. Somehow he managed to free me from the machine and found my legs horribly mangled below the knees and bleeding profusely. Mammy and Mrs Murphy, a woman who was helping her then, rushed from the house with towels and wrapped them around my mutilated legs. Then Daddy turned me upside down and cradled my legs tightly in his arms, putting pressure on the wounds to stem the flow of blood. Swathed in the towels, he carried me into the house and nursed me until our local GP, Dr Nelson arrived. The young doctor, who fortunately was at home when he got word, immediately applied a tourniquet and that staunched the bleeding from both my tiny legs.

My young life was still hanging by a thread, however, as the doctor and my parents urgently discussed what to do next. Unlike today, 1942 was a time of very basic and almost hopelessly stretched health services. Right in the middle of the Second World War, there wasn't even an ambulance available to get me to hospital. So Dr Nelson, accompanied by my parents and a retired nurse, Mrs McCaffrey, set off in his car to get me to the nearest emergency unit at the Fermanagh County Hospital in Enniskillen. Along the twisting, poorly paved roads, the car trundled through Clabby and Tempo, climbing and descending the drumlin hills on the northern shores of Upper Lough Erne, each of the twenty-five miles distance counted off in the fervent prayers of all the adults in that car. Finally, we arrived at the hospital on Enniskillen's Tempo Road and I was rushed off into the emergency department while my parents were left alone to their prayers, their fears and probably their inner self-recriminations.

At that time I was far from out of the woods. I urgently needed a transfusion to replenish all the blood that had been lost from my tiny body. However, there was no such thing as a blood bank back then and my blood group is O Negative, a rare category possessed by only seven per cent of people in the western world and very few of them in Fermanagh or Tyrone. However, if the War meant obvious shortages, it also meant that there was a bigger pool of possible donors among the huge number of armed forces personnel then based for training and deployment in the most western region of wartime British territory; in the lakelands of the Erne valley. An urgent appeal was issued throughout the district, including to the North Atlantic naval protection airbase at Castle Archdale and other places where the forces were barracked. By evening, a suitable donor had been found. Thanks to the generous response of that unidentified person who shared my rare blood group, a tiny girl's life was saved. However, later on that first evening of the day of the accident, the county surgeon Horace Fleming examined me further. The prognosis was not good and my chances of survival required drastic and immediate action. He decided to amputate both my legs from below the knee. I thereby became the only double amputee in Northern Ireland at that time.

I am glad to say I have no conscious memories of the awful accident or of its immediate aftermath. As I grew up and became a parent myself, I realised that my grief-stricken young parents must have been heartbroken and wracked by feelings that they were somehow to blame. My mother was only 22 years old and my father 27 at that time. It must have been an almost intolerable burden to carry as I struggled to survive. I had lost a lot of blood so my life hung in the balance for several days. In the first few weeks following my operation, I was in a state of shock, unable to speak or communicate by any other means. My physical wounds from the accident and the amputation of my limbs were healing, but my mental recovery was an even slower process. Three weeks passed and I remained listless as the hospital staff, family and friends fussed over my bedside. Then Una McCaffrey, the daughter of the retired nurse who had accompanied me on that life-or-death journey to hospital, gave me a doll and I finally uttered my first word, "Baba". The nurses and my family were delighted with that and once I had broken my silence, Surgeon Fleming was confident I would make further progress to recovery.

After that, my general health got noticeably better day by day; so much so that soon, I wanted to go home and, as I was making a little progress, my parents also were keen to take me home. Unfortunately, the short stump of my right leg was still a concern because it was slower to heal than the left due to the number of lacerations it had suffered from the reaper blades. Surgeon Fleming recommended that I should remain in hospital until both leg stumps had completely healed. My parents were naturally anxious about my growing distress. Unlike today, they were not allowed to stay in hospital with a child and with the strict rules applied by hospital matrons of that time, visiting hours were strictly regulated. So those times when my parents could come in to see me were very stressful for all of us.

Finally, after eight weeks in Enniskillen, Surgeon Fleming at last pronounced himself happy with my progress and Mammy and Daddy were allowed to take me home. Their prayers had been answered. Their wee Mary had survived the horrific accident and come home to

Breakley, even if she did so with stumps where her two fine legs had been.

By then of course, the lacerations had gone and the surgical wounds had healed, but the stumps still had to be kept heavily bandaged as they remained tender and painful. Although retired, Nurse McCaffrey offered her services and came to the house every day to look after me. As a child, I called her "Cafferty" and we grew very close because I know that, having helped me to survive such a traumatic accident, she took particular interest in me long after she cared for me as a nurse.

Nor was I far from the hub of family life during that time. My cot was brought from the bedroom into the kitchen. There, one side was let down halfway and tied tightly. I spent a lot of my time in that cot where I was safe and at the same time able to watch the comings and goings of the household. I wasn't yet mobile, however, so I couldn't pull myself up and it would have been too painful to try. Except for Junior Aspirin, there was little pain relief then, so whether it was from pain or frustration, I developed the habit of rattling the sides of the cot until somebody came and lifted me out. Daddy was great for this and he carried me off for walks around the house and even up to the farmyard to see the hens, the pigs and the cows. However, Mammy wasn't able to lift me much because she was expecting a baby – my brother Brian who was born in April 1943. By then I had lots of visitors including family, friends and neighbours. Many of them brought me presents of toys. This was very unusual for a child then, because we normally only received a toy each at Christmas time. My very earliest memory from this time of trauma, distress, love and care is of that cot full of toys.

Then as further time passed, I became more mobile and I recovered the child's instinct to get out and about. I discovered then I could actually go about on my knees, although I had to be careful not to get my stumps knocked. I was getting back to myself as a naturally inquisitive child exploring the world about her. My terrible accident was over, I had no memory of it but my parents were destined to have many a sleepless night with me.

Chapter 2

New limbs

About this time my mother devised a plan whereby I could get about easily with more protection for my stumps. She cut the legs off an old pair of Wellington boots for me. By wearing the feet of the boots back to front I had more protection. So this was how I ran about on my knees up to the time when I was fitted with my first pair of artificial legs. That was in 1944 and I can just about recollect going up to Belfast to be fitted for my first pair of prosthetic limbs. I was four years old and the Clogher Valley Railway had already closed down by then. I remember sitting on Mammy's knee as Daddy drove us to Tynan in County Armagh, in the car he'd borrowed from our neighbours, the Hoppers. There we boarded the train for Belfast. The Second World War was still going on and there were some soldiers in our train compartment. I remember that they made a big fuss over me, giving me sweets, chewing gum and chocolate.

Eventually we arrived at Tyrone House on Ormeau Avenue, Belfast, where the BBC's Broadcasting House is now situated. The three-storey brick building was a very informal centre for artificial limbs, not at all like a hospital. There was a waiting room, a small tea room, a doctor's office, a large room where the limbs were fitted for the male and female amputees (on different days for privacy) and a workshop. I was measured and plaster casts were taken of my stumps.

A pair of leather straps was fitted over my shoulders, and attached to another strap which went around my waist. The lower part of the limbs was made of tin with a pair of leather corsets above the knee. When the limbs were attached to the waist strap I had both support and balance for walking. Our GP, Dr Nelson, told my parents that I should learn to walk without the aid of a stick or crutch and to this day I've never used one.

Since the British National Health Service (NHS) was not introduced until 1948, my parents had to pay for my first pair of artificial limbs. I know that this was quite a financial burden on them with their very limited income from a small farm. Also, of course, there were no state benefits like there are today for those with physical disabilities, so you could say I was a "high maintenance" child!

Despite all the trouble and expense involved, I wouldn't wear my new limbs at the beginning, because I could still get about faster on my own knees. As a small child I found that the artificial limbs were both heavy and cumbersome and I had the added problem of learning to use the straps properly. When I refused to wear my new limbs, Granda Keenan – my mother's father who lived a few fields away in the townland of Corcreevy – would carry me around on his shoulders with my artificial limbs dangling from his hand. He sometimes carried me all the way over the fields to see my grandmother who, as we came into view, would come out to greet us. Like everyone else, my grandparents were finding it difficult to come to terms with what had happened to me but they still indulged me whenever they could. So it took a lot of persuading before I eventually wore the new limbs. I can vaguely remember taking a few faltering steps on our lane, which had plenty of potholes and loose gravel.

Even as a small child, I had to strap the limbs on every morning and take them off every night. This was a routine that I had to get used to for the rest of my life. I also had to wear a pair of woollen socks on my stumps, which always had to be hand-washed. It wasn't long until I became independent, putting on my artificial limbs in the morning and taking them off at night with little or no help from others. Because I was a child who had never known any different, I looked on these artificial limbs as my real legs. My mother, although still very young, was a very sensible woman and she treated me no differently from the rest of the family. Looking back, I now realise this was so important for my upbringing because it taught me independence. Eventually after a lot of practice, I could walk, run, jump and soon I could keep up with my brothers and sisters. By then, I could take part in all our many games.

I learned from a very early age how to use my limbs to my own advantage. When we played Hide and Seek, I could take off my artificial limbs and cover them up, then crawl into a very small space, especially in the hay shed. My brothers would call after me, 'You don't play fair,' but I just laughed at them. Whenever we played Tag, I could stand in a bunch of nettles and, since my artificial legs could not be stung, no one could get at me.

The kitchen was the central part of our house, which had only two bedrooms. In those times, of course, all the day-to-day activities revolved around the kitchen, which also had a pull-out sofa bed and a scullery. Small houses like ours had no living rooms as such. We also had no television when I was a child and the only source we had for news and current affairs was the radio, which in those days was known as "the wireless". As small children we were often told to: 'Wheest, keep quiet till we hear the News,' and our parents listened in to find out if the war would soon end. Mammy had a brother and a sister in London and she worried about them, especially during the Blitz. Some of our neighbours also had friends who lived throughout Britain, so they were also affected deeply by the war.

By the time the Second World War ended, I was five years old and it was time for me to go to school. I was enrolled at Tyreghan National School, which was about one and a half miles from our home and further out into the country from Fivemiletown. My earliest memory of school is that soon after I started, the chestnuts started falling from the huge tree growing at the school entrance. We continued to collect them every autumn when I was at school so we could play "conkers". I'm told that because of Health and Safety rules, this game is no longer allowed on school grounds, which is such a pity. Over the years, I took part in all the games in the schoolyard at Tyreghan – Football, Skipping, Tag, but my favourite was Rounders. I could bat the ball a great distance and that made me a firm favourite among my classmates. The other children never singled me out as being "different", although most of them would have known all about my "tin legs".

There were two rooms in the school. One was for the senior pupils who were taught by Master Sean Cavanagh and the other was the junior room where Mrs Smyth taught. At the front of the two-storey building there was a small porch where we hung our coats, while at the back was a dry toilet. There were no wash-hand basins, soap or water, yet none of us ever seemed to take ill. In the Junior Room where I began, of course, I remember the big black stove that gave out a great heat. Our desks were very close together on a bare-boarded floor and we seemed to be packed in like sardines. Tyreghan National School was a "mixed school", with Catholic and Protestant children being educated together. While the Protestant children went out to play a few times a week, we Catholic children were kept in the classroom to learn our Catechism. We then thought, wouldn't it be great to be a Protestant?

My favourite subjects in school were "Penmanship" and English and I really enjoyed reading. I never liked Sums or Mental Arithmetic and I would quake when Mrs Smyth asked me to recite my tables, especially the twelve-times! There were no calculators in those days.

Both teachers had their own cane, which was used regularly for punishment if we children didn't know what we were supposed to have learned. I remember Mrs Smyth caning me once around the legs; she had forgotten about my artificial limbs, so I felt nothing!

One afternoon a week, Mrs Smyth taught us girls to knit and sew while Master Kavanagh took the boys for nature study. I can remember we learned how to turn the heel of a sock, knit a pair of gloves, as well as all the different kinds of sewing stitches. I sat beside Winnie Clifford in the Junior classroom and Winnie was very good at knitting. So whenever I made a mistake, I slipped my knitting over to Winnie and she fixed it for me. I remember her doing this when we were learning to knit fairisle patterns. I was better at the sewing and Mammy bought me some material and I hand-sewed a frock for my little sister Teresa, who was the youngest at the time. So I found out quite early in life that I enjoyed working with my hands.

In the Master's room there was a big open fire, where we used to heat bottles of milk during the winter months. The coal for this fireplace and for the potbellied stove in the Junior Room was carried into the classroom daily in a big scuttle by one of the senior boys out of Master Cavanagh's class. I remember Jim Nolan and Sammy Gillespie as two of the boys who did this.

We didn't have school dinners provided like there are today in Northern Ireland schools. We had to bring our own lunch, which mostly consisted of jam sandwiches or sometimes sugar sandwiches. There were no school buses either, so we had to make our own way to and from school. My older brother John and I, usually got a lift in Mrs Smyth's car. She lived on the outskirts of Fivemiletown and her children came to school with her. I remember thinking how I would feel if Mammy had been a teacher. That car of Mrs Smyth's, however, seemed to hold an awful lot of children and, while seat belts still hadn't been introduced, back in those days, the cars didn't go very fast anyway. Very few families had their own mode of transport and while some children came to school on bicycles, most walked. In those days, the families were a lot larger that they are today so a few families would have made up most of the school attendance. Some of the family names I remember are Clifford, Nolan, Keenan, Robinson, Carter, Gallagher, Smith, Cavanagh, Stewart and Stanford.

During wet weather, my brothers and sisters wore Wellington boots. So I wanted to wear a pair too, but all the pleading to my mother fell on deaf ears. One day I decided to put on a pair regardless and after a lot of struggling I eventually got them on. It felt great being the same as everyone else but when the time came to remove the "willies", they had to be cut off my artificial limbs. As a child I hadn't realised that the artificial feet were not adjustable or flexible enough to allow the rubber boots to slip off, hence the reason for the drastic action. My brothers and sisters had a good laugh, while Mammy advised me not to try this again. I think she saw the funny side too in my wanting so much to wear the same as my brothers and sisters.

As we progressed up the classes in school, we were transferred to Master Cavanagh's room where a large map of the world hung on the wall. I can recall looking at it and just longing to visit all the great countries, especially Russia which seemed vast and mysterious. The schoolwork in the senior classes was more difficult and we got a lot more homework to do. But for the first time I was introduced to painting and drawing. We hadn't done this in Mrs Smyth's classroom, possibly because there was less room. I soon found I had a natural flair for art. Every Thursday, we had two classes of painting for which the paint came in powder form, from large tins. The powder had to be mixed with water. Hugh Pat Robinson, who sat beside me in the Senior Room, usually gave out the paint and he was always very generous when he came to me, knowing that I was good at art. A jam-pot full of water was also placed on each desk, along with a paintbrush. One day a boy making his way passed the desks to the toilet caught his jacket on one of the jam-pots and sent it crashing to the ground where it shattered into smithereens. The paint and water left a coloured stain on the wooden floorboards. After this incident, Master Cavanagh made a rule that anyone wishing to leave the room had to say, 'Hold onto the water,' and then we had to grip the jars tightly.

I remember one of the older boys shouted out, 'Hold the water,' like a military command and Master Cavanagh nearly jumped out of his skin. In the Senior Room, we also had singing classes. To get our "key", Master Cavanagh used a tuning fork. One song I can well remember learning is "Down by the Sally Garden". Of course, from an early age I was surrounded by music at home, so it didn't take much encouragement for me to learn the piano with my Aunt Kitty. At about the age of eight I began taking music lessons under her supervision. Once I had learned the basics, I sometimes tried to play by ear, but Kitty insisted that I read the music. I went on to pass several music exams with honours.

From time to time our local Parish Priest, Father Nolan, would visit the school. He was small in stature and wore black leggings. He always came to school on an old black bicycle. He did try to drive a car but never succeeded in mastering the skill. During the First World War, Father Nolan had volunteered and was commissioned as an army chaplain to serve in France. He was captured in May 1918 when he stayed behind with some wounded soldiers and was held in a Prisoner of War camp. On his visits to our school, Father Nolan used to tell us stories about this – how poorly they were fed and how they were ill-treated. He also loved to sit down and listen to us singing; sometimes we even sang him to sleep!

There was always an old bicycle about our house. My brother John had learned to ride so he could now cycle to school. I decided that I had to learn also. I was about eight years old at the time. Every evening, I sneaked out with John's bicycle and wheeled it down the lane to the road. Once I reached the incline at Robert Stuart's lane, I could then put my foot on one pedal and, so long as I kept my balance, I could move a short distance. After a few days of this, I realised I had a spectator. Johnny Clifford, a young local farm labourer who lived nearby, had been watching my attempts to ride the bicycle and he realised how determined I was. He volunteered to give me some lessons and did so, right there on the road.

We were fortunate that there was so little traffic in those days, especially so few cars. The only lady driver in the locality at that time was a Miss Kenwell who lived further up our road near the school. Whenever we saw her car approach, Johnny and I kept well in on the grass verge. I also recall Mrs Keenan, a very good friend of Mammy's, who cycled quite a distance to her home balancing two large bags of groceries on the handlebars of her bicycle. She always called out to me, 'Mary, keep at it. Keep at it.' But Mrs Keenan made riding a bicycle look so easy, while I had to keep my balance with Johnny holding on to the carrier. When first I attempted to pedal the bicycle with two feet, I found I was unable to lift my left foot high enough. Such failed attempts lasted for a number of weeks. Johnny had such patience with me, however, and he was always available to give me more lessons.

After all those failed attempts, I began to feel more confident and I knew that Johnny was pleased with our progress. Eventually I did get the "hang" of it and one day I was able to ride off by myself, albeit a bit wobbly. I can still hear Johnny calling after me as he let go of the carrier, 'Keep going. Keep going.'

I then cycled the short distance home where I raced into the house calling my parents, 'I can ride. I can ride.' To show off my new skill for all to see, I cycled up and down the lane. I am sure they were delighted for my sake and for their own, but they never said anything directly. Praise was strictly rationed in those days. However, as a reward for my efforts, I received a new bicycle and this would be my mode of transport for many years to come.

I was now about eight years old and I could cycle to school with my brothers and sisters. I can remember there was a very steep hill just before the school and two good friends Eric and Sammy Gillespie, who were in my class, would push me up the steep incline; it meant I didn't have to get off my bike. I believe shortly after the two boys left school, the family emigrated to Australia.

I owe a great debt to Johnny Clifford for his patience and perseverance in teaching me how to ride a bicycle, because it gave me so much more independence than I would have got otherwise. Looking back to that time, I realise it was the first of many achievements in my life. When an inspector visited our school soon after that, I was asked to take out my bike and ride it around the schoolyard. It only dawned on me in later years that Master Cavanagh was showing the inspector what I could do. At the time, of course, it meant nothing to me because I thought: Sure everyone can ride a bicycle!

Chapter 3
Childhood chores

When I was about ten years old I found I was unable to walk on my artificial left limb because my leg stump was too painful. I had to return to the Fermanagh County Hospital in Enniskillen to be examined by Surgeon Fleming. After this appointment, I was admitted to the hospital to have part of a bone removed, because this was diagnosed as the cause of my pain. That stay in the hospital I remember well and I came to hate the awful smell of disinfectant there. I recall vividly how painful it was having the black gut stitches removed one at a time from my surgical wound because there were no soluble stitches in those days. I also remember my outrage over an incident when Surgeon Fleming took a bag of sweets from my locker and shared them out with every child in the ward, leaving me with just one sweet for myself. However, this was the only time in my life that I had to return to the hospital to have surgery on my stumps.

I remained in hospital for several weeks that time, once more always pining to go home, although the nurses and other staff were very good to me and the other children. Even when I did get home, it took quite some time for the wound to heal and I was unable to wear my artificial limbs until it did so. I was off school for quite a while and I missed spending time with my school pals. Before I could rejoin them, however, I had to return to Tyrone House in Belfast to have a new pair of limbs fitted.

By now the National Health Service had been introduced, so at least my parents didn't have to pay for my artificial limbs after that. That was just as well because I had to have regular running repairs such as the feet recovered or new straps attached and, each time, I had to return to Belfast. The Red Cross car scheme was introduced around that time and a local driver called Sammy Wright would take my mother and me up to Tyrone House in Belfast. Like other volunteer drivers, Sammy was paid an allowance towards his petrol for the journey. This was before the M1 motorway was built so Belfast seemed very far away to a small child. I was a "bad traveller", getting sick regularly on the journey. As a result, I detested those trips to Belfast. But they had to be made and, as I grew older, I had to have new limbs fitted regularly. My new limbs always took a few months to get used to, but after that trip following my hospital stay, I was back up on my bike and away off to school again.

So that I could be up in the morning and dressed as quickly as my brothers and sisters, I decided to keep my artificial limbs on in bed. However, my sister Una, six years younger than me and who shared my bed, had a very poor night's sleep as I kept kicking her. In the morning she complained to Mammy that, 'Mary one didn't take off her limbs last night.' After that, I was checked up on to make sure my limbs were off and beside my bed. I can still remember going to bed as a child back then hoping and praying I would wake up the next day with normal legs, just like my brothers and sisters. But each morning nothing would have changed. Then I would just have to strap on the only type of legs I'd ever have and face another day.

Yet life was as normal as it could possibly be for a child with two artificial limbs. In our large and lively family, I suffered the same trials and tribulations as my brothers and sisters endured. For instance, from time to time my mother would check us all for head lice. First, a large piece of the local newspaper was spread on the kitchen table. The fine comb was produced and the procedure began. I can still feel my mother's strong hand keeping my head in position while she fine combed until my scalp ached. If you moved an inch, you were told to stay at rest and my mother's vice grip was tightened even more. Eventually, when she was satisfied that all was in order, she proceeded to the next victim among her children.

My mother had a busy time trying to keep the house tidy, cook meals and help with the farm work. So we were fortunate in having local girls come to the house to help with the chores. Mary and Patricia McGeary are two that I can remember and they would have platefuls of bread and jam sandwiches ready for us when we finally came home from our adventures. I am sure they were on a very small wage, but we loved to see them coming to help Mammy. They often brought us little trinkets, such as bangles and brooches, little treats that would never have been bought for us by our mother.

My mother was more of a DIY person. She made all her own curtains on an old Singer sewing machine that stood in the corner of the kitchen. She had a keen eye when it came to buying material in the local drapery shop, always looking out for bargains. Because I always wore slacks instead of frocks, they were not readily available to buy. So Mammy would make them on the sewing machine having cut them out using a pattern she had bought somewhere. She also made skirts for my sisters and aprons for herself. After a few layers of wallpaper paste and paint, a strong cardboard box was soon turned into a general holdall which we called the sock box. The socks with holes in them were always thrown into it for darning and it sat under the well-used sofa in the kitchen.

A local woman called Minnie McKenzie also helped my mother every Monday with the large weekly wash. For this, the routine started on Sunday night when the clothes were placed in an old galvanised bath to soak. First, the Rinso washing powder was poured in, and then pots of both hot and cold water were added. A brush shaft was used to pound down the clothes, softening the stains. On Monday morning while on his way home from the creamery, my father was the "chauffeur" who drove Minnie to our house in the horse and cart to do the weekly washing. I can still recall Minnie with steamed-up glasses and with her well-wrinkled hands covered in suds. Sometimes I was asked to give a hand at hanging the clothes on the line. To finish off the weekly chores, the kitchen and scullery floors were scrubbed and Minnie was always very generous with the bleach for that. Going to bed on Monday nights, we would still have the smell of Parazone in our nostrils. In the winter time, a few hard-backed chairs were placed in front of the fire and then clothes, especially woollen jumpers, were draped over the chairs to dry and the steam would fill the house. To this day, I still hate the smell of damp wool.

One of my favourite memories was when John, Brian and myself were allowed to go to the bog to help to save the turf. Once the turf was cut they were spread out onto the bank to dry. When they were eventually dry enough they were then clamped. This was back breaking work with so much bending over to do. We were often more of a hindrance than a help, because as children we loved to run through the heather, trying to avoid the bog holes, while throwing bits of turf at each other. The highlight of the day was tea time which usually consisted of boiled eggs, soda bread and big mugs of tea. We enjoyed helping to light the fire, which supplied enough heat to boil the old black kettle and well worn saucepan for the eggs. Depending on the weather, the turf could be taken home in a matter of weeks. With the load of turf securely built and tied onto the trailer, John, Brian and myself were allowed to sit on the top for the short journey home. Once the turf arrived home, they had to be built into a turf stack

– a skilled job usually carried out by my grandfather. We were now assured of having a good warm fire to look forward to in the winter months.

On Sunday mornings, we could all have a sleep in except my Dad and my brothers John and Brian who had to be up early to feed the cattle and pigs, as well as milk the cows and deliver the milk to the creamery. Daddy would arrive back into the house just about fifteen minutes before it was time to leave for Mass. Sometimes Mammy would have said to us children, 'Run on and we'll catch up.' It's just as well that Father Nolan was never too early starting Mass!

Our mother was nearly always at home of course. The only time I can remember her going into Fivemiletown was to Mass, for a visit to the doctor or dentist or to have her hair permed by Mrs Spears, who owned the local hairdressers on the Main Street. Daddy did most of the day-to-day shopping when he delivered the milk to the creamery. Sometimes after school, however, I would have to cycle into the town to do some errands for Mammy. As I reached for my bicycle with the shopping bag in hand, she would call after me, 'Be sure and get a pound of the good bacon in Bob Parker's, thick cut, and a pound of good ham.'

My Granda McMahon owned "The Valley Butcher's" on the Main Street, so I might have had to purchase some good mince steak there and some beef sausages for Daddy's tea. The only canned foods I can ever remember buying were Heinz baked beans and tinned Bartlett pears. If we were expecting visitors, I might also have had to purchase a Madeira cake in the town. Sometimes I had to go to Sam Martin's drapery shop to purchase a spool of thread or elastic. Very often Sam wasn't in the shop himself so his aunt, Miss Lendrum, would be behind the counter. She held a striking pose in her tailored tweed suit with a fox fur draped around her neck. I always thought that the beady eyes of the animal were staring at me. It was quite scary.

Sometimes my dad would ask me to call into Brunts and get 'a handful of small nails.' Of all the shops, this particular one stands out in my mind. Brunt Brothers was a general hardware shop, selling Wellingtons and other work boots, brushes, and mops, buckets, saws and much more. Some items with handles were hung from the ceiling, mainly buckets. At the back of the counter was an array of small drawers containing different sizes of nails, screws, bolts and other such items. A lot of goods were displayed on the pavement at the front of the shop. The owners, two brothers called Bill and Bob, wore brown shopcoats. Bob always had a pencil behind his ear because all the transactions had to be written down and calculated on paper; there were no adding machines or cash registers in those days. Plastic bags had not been introduced, so all purchases were wrapped in brown paper and then tied up with string from a roll, which was suspended from the roof. It amazed me how they could snap the string with one hand without even using a knife. I just loved to wander around that hardware shop, walking on the old stained floorboards where, over the years, customers' feet had made a well-worn track to the counter.

I tried to plan my shopping trip by starting at the furthest shop and making my way down the Main Street. Then I only had to turn McKeagney's Corner and with a shopping bag balanced on the handlebars, I could then freewheel all the way home.

Once in a while during these shopping trips, however, I would overhear the other customers whispering: 'That's Barney McMahon's wee girl, Mary; the one that had the terrible accident.' I remember feeling hurt as a child when people talked like this behind my back instead of addressing me openly. They seemed to think that because I had no legs, I had no feelings. But I never let my hurt or annoyance show. All the while I would be thinking: I'll show them all one day.

On Saturdays, I enjoyed visiting my grandmother who lived in Crocreevy. I cycled up the Main Street, then down past Ballylurgan Creamery. Once I was on the lane and through a gate that always had to be kept shut, I could begin a marvellous freewheel down a very steep hill that brought me to within a few yards of the house where Granny would be awaiting my arrival. Another girl, Freda Irvine, also visited Granny and both of us would do some odd jobs about the house for her. Freda had been born in the house next door to Granny, before her family moved into Fivemiletown where she went to the town school.

At Granny's, I remember dusting her old-fashioned clock with Roman numerals, under which hung a golden pendulum. It kept very accurate time and had a lovely chime. We had to fetch a few buckets of turf and logs for the hearth fire where Granny did all her cooking. Occasionally, we had to collect eggs and very often some hens would have nested in a ditch away from the house, so Freda and I had to search for their eggs. Granny also reared a few turkeys, so one unusual job we had to do was find some nettles and cut them into small pieces, the cuttings were then mixed into the turkey feed.

Granny's house was quite large in comparison to ours. It had a big kitchen with the open-hearth fire and a small dining room off it. Upstairs there were three large bedrooms. At the front of the house, there was a half-door leading into the hall and the outside walls were always whitewashed, with large pink roses growing up the walls. Freda and I loved to watch Granny making her own soda bread. She never had to measure any of the ingredients because she had done this so many times before. We would sit in Granny's large comfortable chair waiting for the bread to bake in a cast-iron baking pot. We were intrigued as to how Granny could lift the lid which was covered in hot coals without one of them dropping off. After she took the bread from this "oven", we all sat and ate the freshly sliced bread with butter dripping from it and washed it down with cups of strong tea. No other bread has ever tasted as good as this.

On one occasion, Freda and I thought it would be great fun for the two of us to ride my bicycle down the very steep hill on Granny's lane. Freda sat on the seat and did the pedalling, while I sat behind on the carrier. We soon gathered up great speed. Then Freda yelled, 'I can't stop!' We both fell heavily onto the rough stony surface of the lane. Freda came off worst with many cuts and bruises on her hands, legs and face. I only tore the knees out of my trousers and suffered a few scratches on my hands. We tried to explain to Granny what happened but on seeing us, she immediately produced a basin of warm water to wash our wounds. In the end, we found that there was more blood than scratches. Sometimes Miss Lendrum from the shop with the fox-fur collar visited my grandmother and they would chat for ages. I am glad that she did not arrive on that occasion because, if she had seen the state of Freda and me, she would have been very cross with us. Granny did not scold us, however. She was just glad to see that we had no broken bones. And underneath it all, she probably had a little laugh at our escapade. However, as Freda and I made our way home nursing our cuts and bruises, we both agreed that it was worth it all for the thrill we got.

Chapter 4

Fun and Games

With very few exceptions, I was able to enjoy all the pleasures of our life on the farm as the seasons rolled around. During the spring and early summer we had great fun coming home from school, picking wild flowers and eating the raspberries that grew along the roadside. Sometimes we would find a bird's nest and keep an eye on it as the eggs hatched and the "scaldies" fledged and then flew off. Our parents warned us never to touch the nests, just observe. We often filled jam-jars with frogspawn from the "Watery Lane" and watched it grow into tadpoles. Daddy always made us put the tadpoles back into the water so they could eventually become frogs.

During a spell of hot weather, usually in May or June, some patches of tar on the road would melt and my two brothers, John and Brian, would then walk on the soft tar in their bare feet. This happened usually on the way home from school. I would have liked to experience the sensation of melted tar between my toes but this was not possible with my artificial limbs. On arrival at home, the boys would get a good scolding from my mother, who then proceeded to remove the tar with margarine – the only known remedy at the time.

Then with another school year ended and our schoolbags packed away, we looked forward to spending long summer months of freedom. Looking back, I think we had better summer weather in those days. Uncle Johnny always maintained that schooldays are the best days of your life. At that time, we found it hard to believe him and we much preferred the summer holidays to schooldays. We spent most of our time outside during the summer and I remember seeing my brothers and sisters running barefoot through the fields. I wondered then what it would be like to feel the grass on your feet, but I did not dwell too much on things I could not do; I preferred doing the things that I could do. So I just took off my artificial limbs and ran about the fields with my knee stumps in the grass.

A family called the Hoppers lived in the same townland and shared the lane with us. John Hopper was a bread man for the Inglis bakery, and he also ran his own farm. Twice a week as children we took turns to go to the Hoppers' house for the bread. As a child I was fascinated by the size of the bread van, which had special places for all the different types of bread. John used a very long pole to pull the loaves from the inside of the van and Mrs Hopper always treated whoever went for the bread to a few fancy biscuits. For as long as I can remember, we played together with the Hopper children, who went to the Maintained school in the town. Hugh, Margo, Roberta, Beryl and David and myself often played in a make-believe house in the hedge that grew at the side of our shared lane. We used sticks as knives and forks, and any old jars or empty bottles were also put to good use in "our little house" where we used stones for chairs. At the time it was all so real and we spent many happy hours in that "house in the hedge".

Like me, Margo Hopper was the eldest girl in her family, so she had to help out with the usual household chores, such as washing dishes, ironing, minding the baby and shopping for groceries. The one weekly task I hated, however, was washing the eggs. Sometimes scouring powder had to be used to scrub off the dirt. The eggs were then packed in egg boxes and sold to the local shops. For my mother, these eggs brought in extra money for the weekly groceries and other purchases. It was known as the "egg money" and this was my mother's own personal income. Another job I wasn't too fond of was cleaning the windows.

When the weather was fine, the Hoppers and ourselves would make our way down the back fields to a small river known as Killybann. I would take off my artificial limbs and get into the water along with the others. We had great fun throwing stones into the river and making "mud pies". Sometimes we would dam the water with mud and stones to make a bigger pool, and then we would all splash about in it. We usually got so engrossed in our playing that we would forget about my artificial limbs lying on the river bank and by now in quite a dirty state. As "Bumpy", our family terrier dog, emerged from the water and gave himself a good shake, I would be hoping I could get my limbs cleaned up before my mother saw them; otherwise I'd be liable for a good scolding.

During August, our Aunt Kitty came home from London for a two-week holiday. We all looked forward to her visits because she always brought presents for everyone. Aunt Kitty, who was Mammy's sister, was also a marvellous cook and a great help during the haymaking time when there were so many extra hands about the farm to cater for.

One of the highlights of Kitty's holiday was a shopping trip to Clones, which is situated just over the border. There was still a shortage of goods in Northern Ireland and in England in the years after the war. Items such as tobacco and cigarettes, stockings, sugar and much more were scarce and rationed for us. However, they were easily obtainable in Clones, which gave rise to a lot of cross-border smuggling.

A local taxi would be hired to take us to Clones and, while the men had a few drinks in one of the pubs, the women did most of the shopping. There would be pipe tobacco for Granda Keenan, stockings for Aunt Kitty, sugar and tea for my mother and cigarettes for Granny McMahon. Then after meeting up with the menfolk, we would all have a cup of tea and a small snack before heading back "across the border".

I was the only one of the children allowed to go on these "shopping trips", and I soon found out why. At the time, you see, I was one of the youngest "smugglers" on the scene because both my artificial limbs were hollow and that meant they were ideal for hiding "contraband". In my right limb, the stockings were stashed, and then the tobacco was concealed in the left. At the time, I thought it was a great game. When we reached the Customs Post outside the town, the customs man would ask, 'Anything to declare?' I would then look up into his face very innocently. As he patted me on the head, little did he realise I was carrying so much "contraband". The customs men didn't enforce the law too severely and usually when they heard, 'Nothing to declare,' they let us proceed without searching the car. Also, I suppose the fact that we were travelling in a taxi and my aunt had a "posh" English accent, while her husband Willie spoke in strong Scottish tones, probably helped our case. They must have thought we were on a social outing to Clones.

One of the high points of the year was the day trip to Bundoran, the popular seaside resort in Donegal. Daddy would get a loan of his brother Uncle Vincey's car for the day. With our buckets and spades at the ready, we made our way down to the beach where I looked on with envy as my brothers and sisters paddled through the lapping waves in their bare feet. I was not able to join in for this, of course, but Daddy once noticed my frustration. He then took me behind some rocks where I could take off my artificial limbs and he lowered me gently into a small rock pool where I could splash about like all the others. I felt such freedom as the salt-water splurged around my stumps. Eventually, we all had to be coaxed out of the water. That day, as my father lifted me out of the small pool, I could barely dream that one day I would become a competitive swimmer. With my limbs back on again, we all sat on the warm sand and enjoyed a picnic lunch of sandwiches and buns that my mother had prepared. After this we headed off to the Amusements for a few rides on the hobby-horses. We did not spend very long at the Amusements, however as it would have been very expensive for my parents with their seven children.

Another highlight of the year was when Duffy's Circus came to town and the excitement would start as soon as the advertising posters were put up several weeks in advance of their arrival. When the circus arrived a large marquee was pitched in the Commons area of Fivemiletown, while a car with a public address loudspeaker drove around the town inviting everybody to come along. We were allowed to go to the matinee performance and I was given the money to pay the admission for my brothers and sisters. As we made our way up the Main Street, we could hear the circus band playing and there was a great air of excitement as we met up with a lot of our school pals. The circus featured a range of acts – trapeze artists, clowns, bare-back horse riders, jugglers and so on. We sat and watched in awe at what the circus artistes could do. We all loved the clowns. Meanwhile, a woman wearing a sequinned outfit would come around selling ice-cream, and I loved joining the queue to purchase ice-creams for each of us. That little treat made me very popular with my younger brothers and sisters. On the way home, we chatted excitedly about the different performers.

There were other escapades too, in a childhood where I was up for any devilment with the others, unaware that I was meant to be leading the sedate life of an invalid. Our neighbour Robert Stuart had a fine orchard, so my brothers John and Brian and I decided to rob it on our way home from school and help ourselves to a few choice apples. We climbed up a tree but very soon Mr Stuart arrived on the scene. My two brothers climbed down quickly and ran home. They left me still up the tree where one of my artificial limbs had jammed between the branches in my haste to get down. I had to unstrap and take the limb off to release it and then put it back on again while still perched up and hidden by the leaves and the fruit. By then, Robert had left the orchard, so I climbed down and ran home. I am sure now that if we had asked for the apples, Robert would have given them to us. However, it was much more fun robbing the orchard. Even so, when we arrived home and our parents discovered what we had been up to, we got a good scolding.

During the winter months, it could be quite a hazardous journey visiting to the specialist limb-fitting centre at Tyrone House in Belfast, a distance of about eighty miles. So a local electrician Alec Bennock carried out some running repairs on my artificial limbs. Sometimes the buckle of the strap that went around my waist would have broken, so Alec would attach a new one. Or perhaps parts of the feet would be badly worn and he would patch them with the electrician's black tape. I can remember sitting at home, waiting patiently for my limbs to come back from the town, repaired by Alec. These running repairs would have to do until my next visit to the limb-fitting centre.

Winter meant that our outdoor adventures were curtailed; we had to spend more time in the house. We still had the same amount of energy to expend, I remember us running through the house, playing hide and seek, pushing chairs and furniture out of our way as we ran in pursuit of a good hiding place. We tried to be a lot quieter on Mondays and Wednesdays which were the days we got our comics – the Dandy, the Beano and the Topper. Unfortunately, there wasn't one each so there was usually a fight about who got "first turn", very often the dispute was heated and Mammy would have to intervene. She often threatened that she'd stop buying the comics but she never carried out her threat.

Mammy was always devising ways to keep us busy and prevent the bickering that is part and parcel of growing up in a large family. For instance, on Fridays we got homemade chips as a special treat. This meant we had to do all the preparation ourselves. John, the eldest, would go to the garden and collect a bucket of potatoes. Then we washed, peeled and cut them into chips. When these were ready, Mammy cooked them in a large saucepan. It was one meal we all enjoyed eating, possibly because we helped to prepare it ourselves.

We often staged our own concerts during the long nights. The kitchen window was the stage and we took it in turns to disappear behind the curtains and then whip them open for our performance. Our parents gave us lots of rein, maybe they secretly enjoyed our singing and recitations.

Looking back on those idyllic days we had such a happy and carefree childhood. From an early age, I had a very competitive spirit. I can remember my brother John with Hugh Hopper and myself having a bicycle race. It would begin at McNulty's corner, about halfway to Fivemiletown, and finish at our lane – a distance of about a quarter of a mile. I was a bad loser, always wanting to win, and I sometimes did. Cycling was certainly one pleasure that I could enjoy with family and friends and so we cycled many miles all over the Clogher Valley countryside. Back then, there were no convenient snacks such as there are today with plentiful crisps and chocolate bars, so hunger was usually the main reason we went home.

When John and I had all our chores done we were sometimes allowed to go to the small cinema situated at the bottom end of Fivemiletown. Lizzie Reilly always seemed to be in the ticket box. We would only have had the price of the cheapest seats, but whenever the lights were dimmed we sneaked into the more expensive seats.

Most of the time, this would go unnoticed, but sometimes we were caught out, we then had to return to our proper seats! After the film was over, and as John and I cycled home, and we had a good laugh about it! One night as I was going to bed, on taking my limbs off, I complained about how tired my stumps felt. On hearing this, Mammy said in a stern voice, 'Don't run about so much and you won't have that problem.' Looking back, I am glad, and thank God, that my mother never over-protected me.

During the summer it was customary for Mammy to make tea for our neighbouring farmers, Roy and Harry Armstrong, when they came to work at the hay in what we called "Armstrong's Meadow". That was the field we walked through as a short cut when going from our house to Granny Keenan's. Providing the tea for the two young farmers was a token of appreciation for us being allowed to use the short cut. I also really enjoyed taking out the tea and a basket of sandwiches to the men in the field. They sat at the back of the hedge and I'm sure they were glad of the break from their work.

Once they had the tea, the chat would start. I told Harry and Roy about the plans for me to become a "boarder" in Mount Lourdes, the convent grammar school in Enniskillen. I knew that being a "boarder" was not something to look forward to, having learned this from my older brother, John, who had gone off already as a "boarder" to St Colman's College in Newry. Having imparted the news, I lifted the empty basket and the tea can, saying goodbye to Harry and Roy, yet lingering a while to take in the smell of the freshly mown hay. As I set off for home, they called after me, 'Don't worry Mary, you'll do well in your new school.' Then, when I turned into our lane and my sisters Una, Madeline and Teresa came running down to greet me, I realised how much I would miss them all while I was away at my new school.

Chapter 5

Scaling Mount Lourdes

As Mount Lourdes came into view, I could feel a lump in my throat. This was where I would be living as a "boarder" at the Convent of Mercy school in Enniskillen for the coming year and for as many as six more after that in the plans of my parents, who both believed firmly in a good education. To a twelve-year-old coming from the warmth and freedom of a family home in the country, the prospect of attending a boarding school was daunting enough. However, when Daddy parked the old van, he drove back then, and we started to climb one flight of steps, then another, before more flights of stairs, I began to realise why it was called "Mount Lourdes". On my artificial limbs, this would be an additional hardship to rack up with others, following my success in passing the 11-plus. The alternatives, should one not pass the test, was to stay on in the primary system for a few more years before finding work, or to attend one of the alternative schools in the secondary modern system. My brother John had already "reaped" his 11-plus reward when he was sent off as a "boarder" to St Colman's College in faraway Newry the year before.

Boarding at Mount Lourdes meant other changes and preparations. Apart from First Communion when I wore a long dress down to the ankles, I had always worn trousers. They covered my artificial limbs and to most observers, it was not obvious that I had lost my legs. Now I would wear a gym frock, just like the other girls boarding in Enniskillen. Mammy had taken me to a drapery shop there to buy my new uniform. Apart from the gym frock, I needed a coat, blouses, ties, girdle, beret, scarf and gloves as well as indoor and outdoor shoes. These had been packed into a large suitcase as I said a tearful goodbye to my brothers and sisters, including Teresa, the baby of the family whom I knew I would miss most of all.

That first September day at Mount Lourdes, we were greeted by Sister Eucharia, the school principal. She brought us into her office, which had religious pictures and statues all around the place. I still remember vividly the large impressive bookcase that occupied one wall. "Euki", as I soon learned was her nickname, then showed us around the rest of the Convent – the study hall, classrooms, dining hall, dormitories, sleeping cubicles, and finally the Chapel. "Scaling" Mount Lourdes on that familiarisation tour was the first time I had encountered so many stairs, something I would have to learn to deal with in the coming years. I was fairly exhausted as I said goodbye to my parents, yet I felt very lonely and alone on that day. I was twelve years old; visiting was permitted on only one Sunday of each calendar month; and I would not get home until Christmas. As it turned out, however, I had to attend the limb-fitting centre at Tyrone House in Belfast several times while I was in Mount Lourdes. This meant that I went home the previous night and then travelled on to Belfast the next morning. It was lovely to see the rest of my family even for only one night at home. On my return from Belfast, Daddy would drive me back to the convent that night.

There I shared one of the sleeping cubicles with Rosemary Keenan, also from Fivemiletown. She knew about my artificial limbs. In our cubicle, we each had a single iron bed as well as a washbasin and jug, which stood on a bedside locker. Our lockers for outdoors clothes were in the changing rooms elsewhere. That first night I twisted and turned in my bed, unable to fall asleep for wondering what lay ahead of me. One of my foremost concerns was the prospect of having to visit the toilet during the night, not just because it was quite a distance from our cubicle, but because I would have the added bother of putting on my limbs and taking them off again. In the event, I recall this only happened a few times during my entire time at Mount Lourdes.

The routine in the convent was simple but strict. We were up every morning at 7.45 for Mass at 8am. After that, we tidied our beds and then went to the Dining Hall for breakfast, which mostly consisted of porridge. Classes began at 9am and continued until one o'clock when we went back up the three flights of stairs to the Dining Hall for dinner. Here Sister Christina was in charge and it was her job to make sure we were very polite and eating properly at all times. After dinner, it was back to our classes, which finished at 3.30pm. We returned to the Chapel then for the Rosary and after that we had some recreation time. Study began at 5pm with a break for evening tea, then once more up two flights of stairs to bed at 9pm sharp. Once in our cubicles, we had to keep absolute silence with no talking allowed whatsoever. If you were caught breaking this rule, you were punished with a few good slaps of a ruler, usually administered by Sister Vianney.

Her nickname was "Creeping Jesus" and she also taught science, but she was best known for holding her large Rosary beads tightly so they didn't rattle and walking on her tip-toes along the dormitory corridors and around sleeping cubicles, hoping to catch out some of the girls whispering after lights out.

During the course of the week at Mount Lourdes, this was our routine, although there were minor variations along the way. We had no classes to attend on Saturday, so after breakfast, we changed our bed sheets and then dusted and waxed the floor of our cubicles. One of the nuns would then carry out an inspection of this work and God help us if they found any dust. The menu changed too but on a strict rota of meals. Thursday's dinner was my favourite – sausages and chips. I hated dinner on Saturdays, when we had to eat in silence and you could hear the clink of the knives and forks, as the meal was a thin stew. Also on Saturday all the boarders had to walk in pairs up the main street in Enniskillen to St Michael's Church where we went to Confessions.

During recreation after our weekday afternoon classes and the Rosary, we played netball and tennis. At the start of my very first term, I lined up to play netball and I recall that Sister Aquinas seemed very anxious, obviously wondering if I would be able to play. I told her I played football with the boys at home. So Sister Aquinas relented and I got to play netball with the other girls. Her nickname was "Crash" although I never knew how she came to be called this. She was quite plump in stature and, as well as teaching Geography, she was in charge of the games. I remember her as the easiest to talk to of all the nuns and, with her encouragement, I took part in all the games. I was even picked to play on the school's junior netball team. Because of this, I was never singled out as being different from the other girls. Even though I was now wearing the gym frock rather than the trousers I had worn previously, black stockings were a standard part of our school uniform and we had to wear them all the time. On account of my artificial limbs, my mother must have been out a fortune on stockings for me because they lasted me such a short time. The nuns would never allow us to appear with holes or "runs" in our stockings with the result that there were nights before lights out when I had to spend some time darning. Meanwhile, the socks I wore on my stumps were woollen and these had to be hand-washed. So every week I had to send the socks home to my mother with a "day girl" called Mary McKenna. Apart from Mary, my cubicle companion Rosemary Keenan and my closest friends – Dympna McKenna, Edith Cassidy

48

and Pauline Fitzpatrick – I don't even know how many of the other boarders were aware of my artificial limbs. It was simply never discussed openly during my time at Mount Lourdes. While I talked a little about the limb-fitting and how comfortable or otherwise they might be to wear, my artificial limbs were accepted by my friends as just part of my life and they could see that I could cope in Mount Lourdes and take part in everything there.

Perhaps there were other ways that other boarders might have become aware. For instance, every Sunday, except "Visiting Sunday", all the boarders went out for a walk around the island town of Enniskillen. For this, we were supervised by prefects and a few of the nuns. We walked along two abreast for about a mile, with two nuns leading the way and a head prefect taking up the rear. I wasn't able to walk as far as the other girls, so I was accompanied personally by a prefect and only walked part of the way. On the return trek to the convent, the prefect and I could slip into the sweetie shop and "stock-up". My gym frock and pockets would be bulging with sweets I had promised to buy for my friends. We didn't have much money, so I had to get as many sweets as possible for the little money we could scramble together! Once we met two nuns while on the way back to the school and I remember hoping that none of the sweets would fall out from the bulging pockets and crevices I had stuffed them into. The nuns were so deep in conversation they only nodded to us.

I usually had about twenty minutes to spend on my own before the rest returned from the walk and this interval could prove useful in another way. As a special treat for Sunday evening tea, we got a pastry each. Before the others came back, I would sneak into the Dining Hall as promised, and put the choicest pastries on my friends' plates! I always liked the chocolate one; someone else wanted the one with the cream and so on! We could have eaten a lot more but we only got one pastry each.

Meanwhile, I kept up my piano lessons and my teacher in Enniskillen was now Eileen B. Mahon. She was very strict and the music she taught was of a very high standard. Sometimes during the lesson, she would appear half asleep with her eyes closed. Then, all of a sudden, she would hit me across the knuckles of my right hand with a pencil and tell me to keep playing until I got it right. I also studied the violin under the tutelage of Sister Cecilia and played that in the school orchestra, and took part in the school shows and sang in the choir. I loved all this music and the bustle of rehearsing and staging a show or even taking part in choir practice and performances. Coming from a happy but boisterous family home, such activity and noise seemed normal.

However, once a year absolute silence would descend on Mount Lourdes, even during the daytime, when we had our annual school retreat led by priests from various religious orders. This consisted of a lot of meditation, praying and listening to what seemed like endless sermons in the Chapel. The retreat lasted three days, during which time we had to remain silent with no talking, no whispering and certainly no fun or games. I remember little apart from the boredom, except for one priest who told us convent girls that we must go out into the world, get married and have a large family. There were no vocations to the religious life that year!

There were constant reminders of home and family of course. I clearly recall one morning in history class when the smell of burning turf wafted in through an open window reminding me wistfully of home. I was soon brought back to reality when the teacher asked me a question about the First World War.

The fact is that our lives were controlled by the routine and the curriculum. Even our meals were part of the rigid routine and exactly the same menu was served on the same day each week. We had so much learning and studying to do, we found that time passed quickly.

Even so, during that first term at Mount Lourdes, we were counting off the days until we would be going home for Christmas. At twelve years of age, three months is a long time to be separated from one's family. I was looking forward to Mammy's home cooking, especially her soup, apple tarts, treacle bread and good roast beef! The day finally came and, as the other boarders left one by one, I was anxiously looking out for Daddy. Every minute seemed like an hour. When he finally arrived, I just gave him one big hug and the tears welled up in my eyes. We set off and on the journey back through Tempo and Clabby, I kept wishing the old van would go a bit faster, I just couldn't wait to see Mammy, my brothers and sisters, especially John because he and I had a lot of comparing to do about our schools.

Chapter 6
Home for Christmas

It was great to be home again in the warmth of our extended family and I recall so many details of that Christmas after my months of separation at Mount Lourdes. We loved to visit our grandparents and we did so soon after getting home. Aunt Aggie, a sister of Granny McMahon's, was a keen knitter and while she knitted jumpers and cardigans for everyone, Granny did the crosswords. Whenever we called to see them, we were always asked if we knew the answer to some clue. And before we left, we asked Aunt Kitty to play "Robin's Return" on the piano amazed that her small fingers could move over the piano keys so skilfully.

Granny and Granda Keenan were so glad to see us, especially John and me. We had so much to tell them, having both being away at school for three months. They kept asking us about our new teachers, the food and so on. Uncle Frank and Johnny welcomed us as they sat beside the big old hearth fire where large logs and turf burned brightly. My uncles occasionally lifted a coal with a large pair of old black tongs to light a cigarette. In the corner of the fireplace hung the strap that Granda Keenan used to sharpen his cut-throat razor. The old shaving mirror still sat in the back window, where, as a small child, I had often watched him shave. Granny Keenan had a few sprigs of holly placed over the pictures, and across the old dresser. Overall, there was a sense of subdued excitement about the coming of Christmas. It was lovely to see all the shop windows in Fivemiletown decorated with all sorts of toys and games. Next door to Granda McMahon's butchers shop was a sweet shop owned by Joe McNulty whose mother always gave us a handful of sweets.

However, Christmas is quite a busy time on a farm and I had to help my mother with getting ready. There was the plucking and cleaning of the turkey, of course, and the stuffing had to be made and all the vegetables prepared. Mammy always made her own Christmas puddings, which had to be steamed so much, that the kitchen windows misted up. If we didn't have any turkeys of our own for the Christmas market, we had to purchase one from a neighbour. That year, my brother Brian was sent to Lendrum's for the "bird" and he told them we wanted the biggest turkey they had. I don't think he had been sent with that instruction; Brian just liked his turkey!

As a prelude to Christmas, Midnight Mass was attended by the older members of the family and we children all piled into the back of Daddy's van to go to the church while Mammy sat up front with him. The little church was always very cold but, on this special occasion, the large congregation helped to keep each other warm. I accompanied my father up to the choir, where sometimes he sang solo, with backing from the rest of the choir.

Daddy was a wonderful singer and had his voice trained under the direction of Captain Peter Montgomery, President of the Northern Ireland Arts Council who lived in Blessingbourne House, just outside Fivemiletown. Captain Montgomery founded the Clogher Valley Choral Society and the choir included Daddy, as well as my Uncle Vincey, Mick Trodden, Hughie McMahon, Mary Lavelle and Len Stansfield among others. My Aunt Kitty provided the instrumental accompaniment on piano when the Choral Society held a hugely popular annual Variety Concert in the Parochial Hall. We children loved to go to these concerts, especially to hear Daddy's solo performances which were a highlight. Daddy was even compared to the great Count John McCormick and he took part in a Radio Éireann broadcast in an all-Ireland competition for the prestigious John McCormick Cup in which he was the runner-up. From when I was a small child, I remember Daddy gargling with salt and water each day, then practising his vocal chords and breathing exercises. They said you could hear him before you saw him as he was always singing, both in the house and while working around the farm. His favourite songs included "Bless This House" and "The Star of the County Down" and I still recall him practising these with Aunt Kitty on piano. However, my own favourite of his songs was when he broke into "My Mary of the Curling Hair". I always felt he was singing this especially for me.

That year when I came home from Mount Lourdes, I remember Daddy singing "Jerusalem" as a soloist in the church choir. I loved all the Christmas carols, especially when Daddy sang and my other favourites that special night were "Silent Night" and "Away in a Manger". Then as we all dispersed after Mass, I could hear everyone wishing each other "Happy Christmas". To add magic to the occasion, a few flakes of snow began to fall and by the time we reached home, with Daddy singing all the way, the ground was white. After a warm drink, we all went wearily to bed.

On Christmas morning, Mammy was up very early to put the turkey on to cook. She soon realised the bird that Brian had ordered was so big the oven door wouldn't shut, so she had to prop a chair against it until it began to cook and reduce in size. My three younger sisters, Una, then eight years old, Madeline, four, and baby Teresa, just one year old, came on the scene very early to see what Santa had brought, although what we got as children was nothing compared with what they get today. We got maybe a pencil and a jotter with a piece of fruit, or maybe a jigsaw, but not much more.

On Christmas morning we always exchanged gifts with our next-door neighbours, the Hoppers. That year, I received a beautiful gold pen which could write in different colours and I cherished that present for a long time. Then we were back home for the Christmas dinner and Daddy always carved the turkey with a knife he had sharpened carefully on the edge of our stone front-doorstep. As he sliced the turkey, we squashed ourselves in around the table, while Mammy served the potatoes, stuffing and vegetables. I had to help peel the potatoes for the younger ones before I started eating. Then when all were served, Mammy settled herself down on the sofa and ate her dinner from the plate perched on her knee. Because she ate last, there was no room at the table for her and she liked to be free to take care of anyone who needed more of anything. Then when the dinner plates were cleared off, we had Mammy's homemade Christmas pudding with lashings of cream from our own cows, before tackling into the wash-up of a huge pile of plates and bowls.

There had been a heavy snowfall overnight so, as soon as we could after dinner, we raced out to play in the snow. The field in the front of our house had a large hill, where we took turns to go down in our sleigh. Then the Hoppers came along and we had great fun snowballing each other. Unfortunately it fell dark at about 4.30pm and we had to part with our pals, hoping to see each other the next day. In the house, Daddy was preparing to go to the yard; even though it was Christmas Day, the cows had to be fed and milked. The hurricane lamp was lit and Daddy, Brian and John headed off to the yard. John had learnt to hand-milk the cows before going off to school in Newry and he was delighted to milk his favourite cow once more. Brian was given the job of feeding turnips into the pulper, which had a large cast iron drum and a handle. The turnips were put into the drum on the pulper. When the handle was turned the blades inside sliced the turnips, which fell into an old bath placed underneath. The turnips were then used to supplement the feed meal for the cows.

While the boys were busy in the yard, we were busy tidying up the house for the customary visit of our grandparents on Christmas night. The Tilley lamp was lit and, as a treat, I was allowed to pump it. The harder I pumped, the brighter the light, so I was allowed to do plenty of pumping on this special night. There was a good fire burning in the hearth and a hearty supper of turkey sandwiches and Christmas cake prepared.

There was a special cosiness in the kitchen that Christmas night. After all the initial chatting, the pack of cards was produced and we spent a few lively hours playing "Twenty Five". Daddy always seemed to have the Ace of Hearts, the best card in the pack. We were so innocent we didn't know he sneaked it up his sleeve at the start of each hand; we just thought he was very lucky! Eventually we took a break from the cards and the supper was served. Then Daddy insisted on having a rousing singsong with all of us before the end of the night. He would perform his party pieces, of course, and Uncle Vincey, who also had a marvellous singing voice, would give his renditions of "Love Thee Dearest" and "Danny Boy". It must have been midnight before we were sent to bed and the visitors went home.

We woke the next morning to find that there had been a severe frost overnight. Our bedroom window was frozen both inside and out; it was so cold we dressed as quickly as we could and scurried off to the warmth of the kitchen. However, after breakfast we headed out once again to play in the snow. We loved the "crunch" that the snow made underneath our shoes that morning. Then the Hoppers arrived to tell us their pond had frozen over. So with George Hopper keeping a watchful eye over us, we played on it for hours – skating, gliding and falling on the ice. Soon everyone else was complaining about their cold feet but I didn't have that problem.

That magical day soon came to an end as evening drew in once more, but when we were leaving to go home, Mrs Hopper called after us, 'Tell your mother that we will be going to the Pantomime on Wednesday night.' Every Christmas for as long as I can remember, we all went along with the Hoppers to the Pantomime in the old Town Hall in Omagh, a bunch of excited youngsters thrilled to be going over the mountain and through Fintona with John Hopper driving us to the wonderful show, that was such a highlight of the year in Omagh and throughout County Tyrone at that time. Paddy Mossey, Dickie Kennedy, Mary Livingstone and Sheila Taggart were some of those who took part in that wonderful show and, to us, it seemed like a visit to another world. I suppose it would compare today to the annual pantomime in the Royal Opera House in Belfast. This year, it was a great treat for John and me before we returned to our boarding schools.

In the long dark nights of winter, playing cards and Draughts, as well as listening to the radio, were our main forms of entertainment. We had no TV in those days. Cards were played in different houses throughout the locality and the most popular game was "Twenty Five". I loved getting to Keenans' house on their card night because Mrs Keenan didn't take part in the card playing but spent her time preparing the supper which we enjoyed with big mugs of tea to wash it down.

So I cherished the remaining days I had with my family, knowing I would shortly be returning for another term in the large austere convent, which was such a sharp contrast to our small cosy home. The New Year began with little fanfare, unlike today. For us, New Year's Day was treated as another Holy Day with Mass, although I remember we had a big roast beef dinner with all the trimmings. So the remaining time passed and soon I had to call with both sets of grandparents to say my goodbyes before leaving. Then I gave Mammy a hand packing my suitcase and, after a tearful farewell to my brothers and sisters, my parents and I set out for Enniskillen in the van.

The snow had melted and driving conditions were a lot safer on the road as we made our way through Clabby and Tempo to Enniskillen and Mount Lourdes. This time, I knew what to expect there, having already found my way around the convent and its routine. So after another sad parting with my parents, I went up to my cubicle just like all the other boarders arriving back at the same time. After unpacking, we all came down to a light snack in the Dining Hall where we had a good chat about what we had done over the Christmas holidays. We were all in the same boat, missing our families. Later that night after I had taken off my limbs and lay down in my bed, I listened to an occasional sob breaking the silence.

Chapter 7

Back to school

I learned to be resilient at a very early age; dealing with discomfort and at the same time showing a cheerful face. During my years in the convent at Mount Lourdes, some days were very challenging, especially because of all those stairs I had to climb. Standing for a long time was also quite an ordeal, especially during choir practice. Our singing teacher Miss Mahon emphasised that we had to stand to sing properly. I learned never to give in, nor did I want any special treatment. When I occasionally complained about the tough discipline under the nuns, Mammy just encouraged me to persevere and hopefully it would all pay off in later years. This was important to both Mammy and Daddy, because little did I realise then, the financial sacrifices that were being made to keep me at boarding school. At that time, education for most children ended with primary school and there was no real alternative to boarding for us because there were no school buses either.

On returning to school from that first Christmas holiday, we still had the same teachers. However, the lessons now became more difficult and we had to do a lot more studying. I also had to devote time to practising both the violin and piano because Sister Cecilia informed me that I would have a violin exam in a few weeks. This didn't worry me too much as I enjoyed my music lessons. As it happened, I passed that violin exam with honours. I wasn't so successful with other subjects however, especially when I tried to take shortcuts. Our desks in the Study Hall were in rows and although we had a nun supervising us at all times, we could still communicate in whispers and gestures with those right beside us. Bridie Hannigan from Dromore in County Tyrone sat next to me and she was very good at Latin but not so good at Art. Conversely, I was good at Art and very poor at Latin. So we cooperated: I did her Art homework and she did my Latin homework. Needless to say, when exam time came around I failed Latin and Bridie failed Art!

During those winter months after Christmas, the convent was very cold so we all took to wearing a jumper underneath our uniform blouses. However, while other girls complained constantly about their cold feet, I never had to suffer from this! A few of the girls would comment, 'Aren't you lucky?' Little did they realise what they were saying.

The cold was worst in the mornings when the nuns took it in turns to wake us up. Once the lights were switched on, the glare was usually enough to waken us anyway. However, Sister Eucharia was nearly always late for this duty when it was her turn and we would see her running up the corridor still putting on her habit, veil and beads, while calling out at the same time, 'Hurry girls! Hurry!' By the time we emerged from the main building into the cold morning air to attend Mass in the Chapel, the last vestige of sleep would have disappeared as we were chased along by Sister Eucharia with her rattling beads, as she commanded, 'Quick, quick girls. Move along.' We filed into the small convent Chapel, where the nuns sat on either side and we boarders sat in the middle. The wooden floors of the Chapel were always shone to perfection, resulting in the strong smell of polish. Even to this day, if I get a whiff of floor polish, it brings me right back to my convent days.

For morning Mass especially, but indeed all the time, we were expected to appear neat and tidy in our school uniforms. Although there were no irons in the school we had our own way of pressing our gym frocks. We sewed each of the pleats into place with a needle and thread and then carefully placed the gym frock as flat as possible underneath our mattress. We had to climb very carefully into bed and stay as still as possible in our sleep. On removing the thread from the pleats in the morning, there would be a big improvement in the appearance of our gym frocks. We would usually have to carry out this procedure if we knew there was an inspection coming up.

Yet despite the strict and regulated environment of our convent boarding school, we had occasional treats, as well as light moments and a lot of fun. Everyone's favourite treat was the sleep-in until after Mass, which came on alternating days of the week depending on the dormitory section we were in. Even more memorable were the occasional pranks. One day in class, Dympna McKenna's belt became undone. Dympna sat directly in front of me and she was unaware that I had tied her loose belt girdle lace to her chair. Shortly afterwards, Dympna was asked a question and the teacher kept telling her to stand up to answer. She kept trying but remained fastened to the chair, as she whispered under her breath, 'I'll get you for this McMahon!' Despite that practical joke, Dympna and I remained great friends during our years at the convent.

Of all the games we played, I enjoyed netball the most. Even with my artificial limbs, I could run and catch the ball just like everyone else. I was usually picked to play in the striker position because I put the ball into the net most times. Sometimes if my stumps felt tired, I would go to the swings that were situated behind the convent and swing for a short while to rest myself. One day, I lost my balance and fell off the swing. I was mortified with that because usually I didn't ever fall. That tumble resulted in two badly torn stockings and also cut knees. Some of the girls ran off for Sister Aquinas who usually supervised our playtime. She made a great fuss over me, but I kept telling her I was all right. My dignity was more hurt than anything else. On closer inspection, I realised I had broken a strap on one of my artificial limbs. My parents were notified of this and, once more, I had to return to the limb-fitting centre in Belfast for repairs. However, it was great to get home for a sleepover before going off to Belfast.

I remember another incident involving my legs quite clearly. As usual on Saturdays, we walked two abreast up the Main Street to St Michael's Church in Enniskillen for Confessions. We then returned by the Queen Elizabeth Road, a distance of about a mile in total. Then, after having our soul cleansed, the nuns must have thought this an appropriate time to get the bodies cleansed also. We had our weekly bath, washed our hair and changed our clothes. This was a huge operation that lasted throughout the late afternoon and evening as about two hundred boarders took turns using only eight bathrooms. It would start with the senior girls and work its way down to the juniors, although sometimes the entire operation had to be stopped for a long interval to allow the water to heat up again. The bath was only filled a few inches deep and this was always checked by the supervising nun. Even so, by the time we juniors got our turn, the water would often be only tepid so there wasn't much temptation to linger.

On that Saturday evening, I had just got out of the bath when my head became very light. I fainted then. I don't know how long I lay on the floor, but it must have been quite a while for, when I regained consciousness, I could hear Sister Majella and Sister Aquinas shouting, 'Mary! Mary! Are you all right?' I was not all right, but I wasn't prepared to let the nuns see me without my artificial limbs. So I called back that I was fine, while I struggled to get my limbs attached and get myself dressed as quickly as possible. By the time I came out of the bathroom, the nuns had gone, so I was able to get to my sleeping cubicle without any fuss. Although Sister Majella and Sister Aquinas never embarrassed me by mentioning this incident, the locks were removed subsequently from all the bathroom doors. Some of the senior girls weren't too happy about this. I gathered that my fainting incident prompted this new arrangement but I kept quiet about it also.

There was one other major dramatic moment from that first year in Mount Lourdes. During breakfast one morning, Sister Eucharia swept into the Dining Hall with a face like thunder. All of a sudden, everything fell quiet. We didn't need to be told that something serious was amiss. Everybody tried to guess. Had someone had a serious accident? Did someone die? Or did someone steal something? With bated breath we waited for Sister Eucharia to speak. She then called out the names of five senior girls and instructed them to remain in the Dining Hall after breakfast. We still didn't know what was happening. However, one of the named girls happened to be the head of our table. Her face had gone completely white and she looked very worried. When the day girls arrived for class, all was finally revealed. The five senior boarders had sneaked out of the convent to a dance and this became the main topic of our conversation for days to come.

Over time, we shared the details of how the five boarders had climbed out through a ground-floor classroom window and made their way through the grounds to the home of one of the day-girls in the town. There they changed into frocks and put on some make-up and headed off to the dance in the Town Hall. Later they made their way back, changed into school uniforms and entered the school by the same window. However, they had been spotted and recognised by some nosey look-out in the town who couldn't wait to tell the nuns the next day. We also learned that after a severe reprimand from Sister Eucharia, the culprits were expelled forthwith and were only allowed to return to Mount Lourdes to sit their final exams. It is only fair to point out that these boarders were all young women of eighteen or more at the time. Yet we were all so meek then, that nobody would have pointed this out. However one thing is certain, after this episode, no one ever tried to sneak out again.

Spring rolled on into summer and, the next thing we knew, it was the end of June and we were heading off home from school for a whole two months. Once there, the schoolbags were dumped in the scullery, not to be opened or even thought of again until September approached.

Chapter 8

The Magic of London

I was wearing my new frock and clutching a small handbag containing the pocket money given to me by neighbours and other family friends. I hoped the Maguires would not be late collecting me for the night-time journey to Belfast to catch the early morning ferry to Liverpool. Excited about my first trip outside Ireland, I was also very anxious about getting to London and Aunt Kitty who had invited me over for a holiday as a reward for completing my first year at boarding school in Enniskillen. Gerry and Anne Maguire arrived on time, I said my goodbyes to Mammy and Daddy, then dozed through the drive to Belfast. Before I knew it, we were at the ferry dock, watching young men and women saying final farewells as they set off in search of work in England. These people were part of the huge wave of Irish people who flocked to England in the post-war economic boom of rebuilding ravaged cities and creating a modern industrial economy. Even as they embarked on their dreams of a new life across the water, many of those travelling in family groups must have known they would never return home. Even as a young girl, I could sense the sad finality of their boat journey back then.

I was determined not to get lost myself, so I stayed close to the Maguires. Together we searched for seats and found a quiet spot just as the ship pulled off and moved down Belfast Lough. Once I knew where the Maguires were, I went off to explore. However, I found it difficult to keep a balance on my artificial limbs as the boat rose and fell in the gentle swell of Belfast Lough. The rocking motion was quite unsettling, but I managed to find a convenient vantage point and watched the city fade into the distance.

For the rest of the crossing, passengers milled about between the bar, the restaurant and the various decks. We had a bite to eat, more to pass the time between sleeping and chatting than because of hunger. I was restricting my movement because of uncertainty about staying upright on my own artificial "sea legs". However, when we docked in Liverpool, I heard several people remark that it was a "pleasant crossing". We boarded the waiting train and soon we were off on the overland journey. I remember noting how similar the countryside was to Ireland, but I also took in the subtle differences that reminded me I was getting farther from home. The towns and villages seemed tidier and bigger, the countryside less populated in between. I remember that it was quite stuffy in our compartment in the summer heat and a man was sitting opposite doing a crossword, quite oblivious to the attempts of a young woman beside him trying to control her two children. We got tea and sandwiches from the dining-car, but soon the children had fallen asleep and, lulled by the motion of the train, we dozed.

I don't really recall my first impressions of London, just a voice calling, 'Last stop, Euston Station.' I alighted from the train groggily, but there waiting for me on the platform was Uncle Willie with a big welcoming smile. I felt safe and sound at last as he took my case in one hand, my hand in his other and we set off striding confidently through the confusion. And so we were soon on the final stage of my great journey, going by bus to their home at 22 Gloucester Avenue, off Regent's Park Road.

Aunt Kitty was waiting for us and she reached for my suitcase to show me to my room. It slumped to the floor. 'What on earth do you have in your case to make it so heavy?' she asked. I then remembered the cooked whole chicken Mammy had packed among my things to ensure I would not arrive empty-handed. Buried among my things, it could well have remained there, forgotten and rotting in the summer heat of July in London. So we settled down to a plentiful tea as I was quizzed for news of home, of school, of family and I was told of what to expect here in London, the centre of the world.

The lovely old three-storey house in which Aunt Kitty and Uncle Willie lived had withstood the Blitz of the Second World War that had flattened many other parts of London and elsewhere in Britain. There seemed to be large rooms everywhere in this house shared by that loving, but childless couple, unlike our cramped and noisy home. I was particularly enraptured by the beautiful stained-glass window on the landing. From a window at the rear of the house, I could watch steam trains going by on the rail lines to Euston Station. I had never seen so many trains before and was fascinated by their size and the great steam they let off. I remember one was called "The Flying Scotsman" and I presumed it went up north to Scotland.

After we had eaten on that first day of my London holiday, I was introduced to Miss Phelps. She was both a friend and landlady to Aunt Kitty and Uncle Willie. She immediately set about ensuring that my holiday would be one to remember in every aspect and she seemed to know exactly how to go about that. For a start, Miss Phelps was able to get a special pass for us to go and see the horses and carriages in the stables of Buckingham Palace. This wonderful tour included seeing the magnificent Gold State coach, in which the young newly crowned Queen Elizabeth II of England had been transported on parade, after her coronation only the previous year and the equally impressive Irish state carriage which carried the Queen Mother and Princess Margaret on that huge occasion. Our tour also brought us to Trafalgar Square, Hampton Court Palace, Westminster Abbey, St Paul's Cathedral,

Madame Tussauds, the Houses of Parliament and the great art galleries of London.

I learned that Miss Phelps had once been married, but after a few months she decided that it wasn't for her. So she up and left her husband and, if she had ever adopted the title of "Mrs", she reverted to insisting on being called Miss Phelps. She was a private school teacher and one of her pupils had been the well-known actor Peter Sellers. After the Second World War she set up her private school at 22 Gloucester Avenue, where Aunt Kitty and Uncle Willie had their large flat, comprising of a living room, kitchen, two bedrooms and bathroom, as well as the use of other rooms in the house.

Miss Phelps, meanwhile, was far from a stereotypical prim schoolmistress. She loved to have a flutter on the stock market and very early each morning, she set off on foot through Camden Town to the local market, coming home laden down with fresh vegetables and strawberries. During the hot summer weather, she shared a basement dining room with her two tenants – and their young guest from Ireland, of course – because it was much cooler. After dinner, she loved to play Bridge and during the few weeks I was there, she went to great trouble to teach me the card game so I could take part.

At that time, Aunt Kitty was the manageress of Lyons Corner House on the corner of London's Tottenham Court Road. On one occasion, Miss Phelps and I had tea there and it was my first time to taste a Knickerbocker Glory ice cream. Of course, Aunt Kitty made a great fuss over me and introduced me to all the staff, some of whom were foreign and could speak very little English. Because of her job, Aunt Kitty had frequent contact with the Royal Family and its household. She managed the catering for the garden tea parties hosted by the Queen Mother and they met frequently and were on friendly terms. After these tea parties, Aunt Kitty would arrive home exhausted and only relaxed when she had her aching feet soaking in a basin of hot salted water. When I saw her do this, I wondered what that would feel like, knowing that I would never find out.

On our wonderful outings to see the sights of London with Miss Phelps or Aunt Kitty, I had to do a lot of walking in the very hot weather. There were a lot of pressure sores on my stumps as a result and the only way I could counteract this was to cover the affected areas with Elastoplasts. I had to do this without Aunt Kitty's knowledge, otherwise she would have wanted me to rest up. But I persevered because I was having such a good time and I didn't want to miss out on anything.

I soon adjusted to the pace and size of the city, although I was amazed at the noise of the traffic, so many people hurrying by, so many buses going here and there. My Aunt knew the numbers on them and knew what routes they took to places that sounded magical to the ears of a young convent girl who had grown up on a quiet farm in the Clogher Valley. I liked to ride on the double-decker buses, especially on the top deck, but it took some time to get used to the noise and bustle of the traffic. The Underground rail system, called "The Tube" was another novel way to get about and the escalators were great because they moved you along, with no need to walk on artificial limbs attached to bruised and bandaged stumps.

For her part, Miss Phelps had never met an amputee before, so she was keen to see my artificial limbs and how they operated. She was fascinated at how quickly I could put them on and she also remarked that they were quite heavy. I didn't pass any remarks about showing my artificial limbs to Miss Phelps. Yet she was the very first person outside my own immediate family to see my artificial limbs being attached and taken off. I was rarely asked about them, so Miss Phelps' curiosity was probably refreshing and I didn't mind it in the least.

There were really special moments on that wonderful holiday. I remember on one occasion, Aunt Kitty took me along with some of her friends on a day outing to Brighton. On the way down on the coach we all sang "Enjoy Yourselves (It's Later Than You Think!)", that wonderful song which was hugely popular back then. We had a great time sitting on the world famous Brighton pier, eating ice cream and soaking up the summer sun.

Because she didn't have any family of her own, Aunt Kitty really pampered me for those few weeks. I liked to watch her putting on her make-up; she always wore a red lipstick and sometimes she allowed me to use it. On one occasion, we attended a show in the London Palladium where I saw a performance by Norman Wisdom and that was certainly one of the highlights of my trip. On another night out in the Haymarket theatre, we went to see the live show of "The Sound of Music". That was about ten years before it was transformed into the magical musical film that still captivates audiences today.

Before returning home, Aunt Kitty also brought me around some of the popular London department stores to view the latest styles. I was amazed by the size of these shops and I just loved the escalators, which saved me the trouble of climbing stairs on my artificial limbs. I remember thinking that Harrods was as big as all of Fivemiletown and I wondered who could even afford to shop in such an exclusive place. I knew for certain that neither Aunt Kitty nor Miss Phelps did. My favourite shop was Marks and Spencer where I really admired the smartly presented shop assistants with their carefully applied make-up. Because we always purchased our clothes in Fivemiletown on "tick", I wondered if the huge stores in London did the same and then wondered how they could keep a ledger big enough to list all the families in the city! Yes it was cash purchases when we were there and through the warm generosity of Aunt Kitty and her friend Miss Phelps, I ended up with lots of new clothes to bring home.

I remember my last day in London, listening for the church bells to signal my time to set off for the train to meet up, as prearranged, with another couple heading home for holidays in the Clogher Valley. I had already heard the chimes of Big Ben up close, and thinking this was wonderful because I had only heard them before on the radio at home. I had entered a world that was vaguely familiar, but unreachable, for so many people back in Fivemiletown and my Enniskillen boarding school. Now I was heading back with lots of wonderful stories to tell about all the places that I had visited in London.

Chapter 9

The Teenage Years

After four years at the convent, I did not want to return when I turned sixteen. I had received a good education at Mount Lourdes and that stood me in good stead for the rest of my life. My parents were understandably disappointed that I did not wish to continue at the grammar school, which they regarded as a vital passport to professional training and independence in life, especially for a double amputee whose future prospects were uncertain. However, my mind was made up and they came to realise that my time in boarding school had been very strenuous for me, both physically and mentally. I stayed at home for the next few years, helping my mother with the housework, but I continued to keep up music lessons with my Aunt Kitty (my father's sister) in Fivemiletown who had started me on the piano before I moved on to Miss Masterson, a qualified music teacher who prepared me for examinations.

During this time, my mother had to spend a few weeks in hospital and several more weeks recuperating at home. I then had to take on the day-to-day running of the house. This involved all the cooking, washing, cleaning and looking after my younger brothers and sisters. I would make up their lunches for school and have a meal prepared for when they returned home. I remember vividly my first attempt at making gravy by following the instructions on the Bisto packet; there were no granules in those days. Unfortunately the end result was far from the flavoursome gravy Mammy could make without any instructions. I really couldn't wait for her to get back to full health again, because while I didn't mind helping out, I found housekeeping both tiring and tedious. However, nobody in the house complained and my Uncle Johnny actually complimented me on my lovely cooking.

Uncle Johnny, who spent a lot of his time with us, was a man of quiet wisdom and a drôle sense of humour. He had a great love of animals and he owned two dogs that were his constant companions. Once when Daddy caught a fox in the farmyard, he was bent on killing it as vermin, just as any farmer would have done. However, Uncle Johnny wouldn't allow this and a compromise was reached. It was put into a barrel covered by a sheet of tin with a large stone on top to secure it. They would decide in the morning what to do with the fox. When morning came, of course, the cute fox was gone. Mammy was livid when she heard this because she had chickens and she had lost several to foxes over the years. But nobody could be cross for long with Uncle Johnny. He had his own gentle way of looking at things.

A local man who used to "ceilidh" (visit) in our house was a bit of a "know-all" who could have outworn his welcome many a time. Uncle Johnny nicknamed him "The Oracle" and that softened our view so much that we even began to look forward to visits by "The Oracle" to see him live up to the name Uncle Johnny had given him. He also softened the consequences of rash youth too. I remember one time when, in a rage over something, I flung a basket of eggs to the ground smashing most of them. Immediately I realised that I had wiped out some of Mammy's precious "egg money" for that week. I stood looking at the smashed eggshells, not knowing whether to laugh or cry. Uncle Johnny arrived on the scene and he said quietly, 'I'll take the blame.' And he did, although Mammy knew quite well that he wasn't to blame. Having no proof, there was nothing she could do and, once again as so often before, Uncle Johnny had covered for one of us children he loved so dearly. Now that I had left school and was trying to assert my independence from my parents, Uncle Johnny provided constant support and encouragement as I tried to work out what I wanted to do.

During the winter months, it was customary for the men to "ceilidh" with their neighbours, and farming provided the main topics of conversation. We loved to see the neighbours coming because they usually brought us a bag of sweets. I recall Jimmy Stewart, Roy and Harry Armstrong, as well as Pat and Peter Cullinan being regular visitors to our house. When Jimmy came by, he would often trim Daddy's hair. He then offered to do the same for my brothers but the old trimming machine he used was not very sharp. This resulted in an occasional "yank" to the scalp! When my brothers heard about Jimmy's next visit they were nowhere to be found.

A constant visitor was Hughie Nann who worked on our farm for years having been orphaned at a very young age. He had brothers and sisters but didn't see them after the family was split up. One night in a pub he was introduced to a brother whom he didn't even recognise. Hughie loved to listen to the wireless, especially the news and the weather forecast. He used to say, 'Ah Missy,' – which was how he addressed our mother – 'will you tell them childer' to wheest 'til I hear the news?'

For those couple of years after school, I was still considered one of the children, although regarding concessions going out to dances and other events, I had little money to do so. One of the family rituals of that time in our house, as in Catholic homes throughout the country, was saying the Rosary. At the appointed time in the evening, everyone knelt down at chairs or the sofa to take part in the praying which took about twenty minutes. Daddy would then begin: 'Thou oh Lord will open my lips.' We all then took it in turns to say a decade. Sometimes as children we began to giggle and laugh, only to be given a good smack by Mammy. Then with the Rosary finished, which only took about ten minutes, Mammy began the trimmings in which she seemed to pray for half the country – friends in hospital, deceased members of the family and souls in Purgatory. I was exempt from kneeling down because of my artificial limbs, so I had a fine view of the proceedings. This usually involved all the nudges and silent giggles as my brothers and sisters tried to liven up the boredom by having someone else scolded. Any interruption of proceedings was always welcome and on one memorable occasion, this was provided by the house cat.

Back then, bedroom slippers were a luxury virtually unseen in country homes. At night, men simply kicked off their boots or shoes and sat around in their "sock soles". Daddy loved to sit in his chair at night, warming his feet at the fire while wearing the heavy woollen hand-knit socks we gave him as gifts at Christmas. On the night in question, he was kneeling in his customary position, his head buried in prayer, oblivious to the shenanigans going on behind his back. I could see his big toe protruding from the top of the sock where his right foot rested across his left ankle. He was keeping tempo with the prayers by wriggling his big toe, making it more and more exposed through the hole. The cat, which had been sleeping in front of the fire, woke up and spied it there, wriggling and enticing her. For a full decade of the Rosary as I looked on, the cat stalked her quarry. I was mesmerised by her manoeuvres. She would creep closer on her belly, then jump back as if electrocuted when the tempo of the toe changed suddenly, creep back, move to a different angle, all the time watching the toe and preparing for her final move. It came when she moved stealthily on her belly from three feet to one foot away, reared up on her haunches, set back her ears and sprang with all her might on the prey, burying her teeth and claws to the hilt in the soft flesh of Daddy's big toe.

The reaction was immediate, furious and epic. Daddy rose from his knees like a colossus, flung his Rosary beads aside and his face was like thunder. Although a big man, he turned with the speed of lightning and issued the irreverent exclamation, 'Ye damned auld bitch.' With that he caught the cat by the scruff of the neck, charged to the front door, which he flung open and dispatched the animal off into the darkness as far as he could throw it, with a torrent of expletives I could barely believe my father would know, never mind utter. By the time he returned to the hearth, limping on his wounded toe, the Rosary was truly over for that night!

Once I had reached my teens, meanwhile, I no longer wanted my mother to accompany me to the limb-fitting centre in Belfast. Instead, Jean Woods, a cousin who was a few years younger than me and still at school, came quite a few times. I remember one occasion when Jean had a lovely new red coat. While cycling over from her house just outside Fivemiletown, the tail of her coat got caught up in the bicycle chain and it was covered in black oil when she managed to free it again. However, Jean was so excited about going with me to Belfast that she was not too bothered about her new coat. Our driver Sammy was very good and, after my appointment at the centre, he allowed us to look around the shops in Belfast. As a teenager, I was becoming more aware of my appearance and so this was a great opportunity to see the latest fashions in the city.

During the summer around this time, I noticed that my artificial limbs looked paler than everyone else's real legs. So I purchased a small tin of paint so that I could make them a more natural colour. It didn't take very long to colour the two artificial limbs and I then waited anxiously for them to dry. My mother came on the scene and she admired my handiwork. Then with my limbs back on again I was delighted with the result and I believed that I didn't stand out from the crowd.

As a teenage girl, I had a head of thick straight hair, so my mother suggested that I have a perm. I can remember clearly emerging from Mrs Spear's Salon in Fivemiletown with my new hairstyle. It may have kept my mother happy but I didn't very much care for it myself. Anyway, there was nothing I could do about that. I just had to learn to live with it knowing that it would grow out sometime.

Our small house was always full of fun and laughter on Sunday evenings as family and friends gathered. After the family Sunday dinner, my mother would go up to bed for a few hours for a well-earned weekend rest. After reading the Sunday papers, Daddy would usually doze off in his favourite armchair beside the fire. It was then customary for a few friends and cousins of our own age to visit us in the afternoon. These included Patricia and Eileen and Elizabeth McMahon from Fivemiletown, Rea Mullan and Mary and Dympna Keenan. We liked to try out new hairstyles together, back-combing into the style that was known as the "Beehive". It was all the fashion then. I got to practise backcombing on them all. In particular, Rea had thick hair that was ideal for backcombing and it really stood up with little encouragement and then held its shape. Like everything else in those days, a lot of preparation had to be done before we got down to washing the hair. The only means of having hot water was from the kettle which would have to be boiled quite a few times for the hair-washing. Then after applying plenty of setting lotion, I would put the rollers into the wet hair. While we waited for it to dry, we liked to experiment in the kitchen; trying our hand at making meringues, which meant beating the whites of eggs well and then adding plenty of sugar. We took it in turns to beat the mixture with an old hand-mixer. When we thought it was all right, we made small nests on a baking tray and placed that into the oven. We then tidied up, cleaning and

77

putting away our cooking utensils. With a cup of strong tea, we then sampled our meringues. My father, who had a sweet tooth, would usually wake up about then and have a few also.

After that, we usually took a stroll with our visitors up around the fields and into the farmyard to see the animals. We always had contradictory views of an ideal life: I thought it would be great to live in the town, while my friends thought living in the country was great. However, our interests as teenage girls were the same no matter where we lived and on those Sunday afternoons we also spent a lot of time deciding what we would wear to a local dance, providing we got permission to go to it. There was a method we employed in asking this. First I would go to Mammy and she would ask, 'Did your father say you could go?' That began the toing and froing and eventually somebody would give me permission. Because Uncle Jim, my father's bachelor brother, was both our driver and chaperone for these dances, our parents knew we were in safe hands.

Sometimes if Uncle Jim wasn't available to drive us to the dance, a local friend called Benny Gallagher would give us a lift. We would all pile into Benny's little Austin A30 car and sit three deep in the back seat. Despite the cramped space, we had such fun going to and from these dances.

Short pencil skirts which came just to the knee were in vogue at the time and all my friends wore them to the dances. I realised that if I wore a short skirt too, it would draw too much attention to my artificial limbs, which I always tried to disguise as much as I could manage. I preferred fuller skirts that came below the knee-straps because that would cover my stumps, and even better I would have loved to wear slacks, but it would have been unheard of for a girl to wear trousers to a dance back then. However, at these small country dance halls in places such as Cooneen and Derrygannon, most of the young people present would have been my school pals, so they knew about my tin legs. In any case, I wasn't too bothered because I could dance just as good as any of them.

We all did the "Jive" back then and we practised it at home and in school before venturing off to the dances. Back then, of course, the dances all followed the same routine from the big ballrooms in the cities and big towns to small parish halls in remote rural places like Derrygannon. The men congregated on one side of the hall, while the women sat or stood at the other side. Sometimes it could be quite a while before anyone among the men was brave enough to venture out for the first dance. Once he did, there was a stampede across the floor by the other men. Often the intended dance partner he had been eyeing up was already out on the floor by the time the man arrived, leading to an awkward exchange as he made a second choice. I suppose for that reason, the Ladies' Choice dances were very popular, even with the shy men.

Chapter 10

Starting my career

My brother John had finished his A-Levels at boarding school in Newry and he had gone back with Aunt Kitty (my mother's sister) to London to seek employment there. This was the first permanent break in our family unit and we were sad to see him leave knowing that he would no longer be coming home at the end of another term from St Colman's. At the same time, we were also confident that with a good education from there, he would have plenty of opportunities in London. He found a good job in Smithfield Markets and he soon became the manager of a thriving business in the meat trade, continuing the McMahon tradition of his grandfather. After John left, I also became restless. For although I was happy enough to stay at home and help out with the day-to-day running of the house, my ambition was to gain employment and become independent. I knew my parents wanted this for me too. I had no clear career path in mind at this time, but I knew that I wanted to work with people using my skills in both Music and Art.

The social worker for "the disabled" in the Omagh area at that time was Eilish Gallagher. She suggested that I should consider becoming an occupational therapist. At the time, I didn't even know what that meant, but after she explained the kind of work involved, I knew that this was the type of job I would like to have. So she arranged a visit to the Occupational Therapy department at the Tyrone and Fermanagh Hospital, the large psychiatric care facility in Omagh. There were between forty and fifty patients in the department on the day we called, all busy doing different kinds of craftwork. I found it very easy to approach the patients and they asked lots of questions: "What's your name?", "Where do you come from?" At this time, of course, I didn't know any of the patients and they didn't know me. Yet as we said goodbye to the Occupational Therapist, Pat Hodson, I knew for certain that this was the type of work for me.

A few months after our visit to the O.T. department in Omagh, Eilish Gallagher told me she had heard that, because of the shortage of qualified occupational therapists, the National Health Service was planning to appoint assistants who could be trained within the hospitals. I applied immediately, and in my application said that I had visited the O.T. department at the Tyrone and Fermanagh Hospital and believed I had the right aptitude for this job. Some time later, I was called for an interview before a panel consisting of two doctors and the Matron. I was quite nervous but they soon put me at ease and I hoped I had an advantage in telling them that I had already visited their O.T. department. My interview was successful and I was offered the position of assistant occupational therapist starting on 1 June 1958, just as I turned eighteen years old.

My parents arranged lodgings for me with the McCormick family in Cranny and they paid rent in advance for my first month's keep. When they said goodbye, I felt I was literally left standing on "my own two feet". The McCormicks lived in a large farmhouse and all the family were grown up and married, except for one son called William. He was about fifteen when I stayed there and he helped out on the farm, milking cows and looking after the calves. It was very convenient for getting to work, as it was only half a mile from the hospital.

That first Monday morning I cycled to work and I was full of trepidation about what lay ahead. I knew I had an awful lot to learn and I wondered how the patients and staff would accept me. Long after I retired, having worked there for thirty years, I learned that the other staff members were as nervous about meeting me, a double amputee, as I was about joining them. They expected me to be walking with elbow crutches or a stick. They were quite surprised when I walked in on my own. Some of the older staff nurses were actually amazed at seeing me. They remembered hearing about my accident at the time that it happened and they were all under the impression that the wee girl whose legs were cut off by the mowing machine had succumbed to her injuries and died. So they commented openly about how I walked "normally" and how well I had adjusted to wearing artificial limbs.

I was greeted on arrival at work that first day by Pat Hodson, the Occupational Therapist I had already met on my first visit. She would now be responsible for my training as an assistant occupational therapist over the next three years. I then had to report to Robbie McKinley who was in charge of the salaries and wages. He informed me that I was being issued with a "blue card" – this meant that I would be registered as a "disabled employee". I remember this vividly as the first time in my life that I was referred to as "disabled". I was taken aback because I had never considered such a label being applied to me. This word had never been used in my hearing, either at home or at school. Now here I was starting a job in which I would be carrying out exactly the same duties as other staff members who were "able-bodied" and I was being tagged with being "disabled", as if I was only there to meet some quota set by the government. Shaking from this meeting with Mr McKinley, I then reported to the Chief Male Nurse's Office where I was issued with one large "Female" key and one "Male" key. These would allow me to gain admission to the Male and

Female closed wards. As I was leaving the office, I was warned, 'Lose your keys and you lose your job.'

Pat Hodson then took me on a conducted tour, during which I found out that there were lots of stone stairs to climb. The main part of the hospital was a grey stone Victorian building, three storeys high with lots of small windows. At that time there were 1,200 resident patients and a total of 1,425 staff to run the facility's twenty wards, each having between forty and fifty patients. The male patients were accommodated on one side of the hospital and the females on the other. There were two "front" offices, one occupied by the Matron, and the other by the Chief Male Nurse. In those days, patients were categorised for short-term, medium-term and long-term care. The majority at Tyrone and Fermanagh Hospital were in the long-term category.

The Tyrone and Fermanagh Hospital was also a teaching hospital and there were two large classrooms on the second floor, which the student nurses attended under the supervision of Miss Dolan, the Head Tutor. I would be joining them for some of this instruction. On the ground floor there was a large recreation hall, the staff canteen, patients' canteen, a "tuck shop", a very large kitchen, a laundry unit, a large store, cobblers shop, a barber shop and a ladies hair salon, the boiler room, nurses' accommodation and the salary and wages office.

While the Tyrone and Fermanagh Hospital was one of those huge forbidding grey Victorian buildings in which psychiatric patients were confined and treated back then, the surrounding grounds were covered in beautiful shrubs and large mature trees. There was a tennis court to the front and also the Gate Lodge where the maintenance staff – painters, electricians, laundry workers and others – "clocked in" each day. Also, just a few yards from the main building was the residence of Dr Johnston, the consultant psychiatrist at the time. He was generally known to all the staff as the "Super". Also on the grounds were other buildings including a small church and a "chapel" to cater for the different religious denominations and the Mental Health Extension or M.E.H. The later was jokingly known as "Mickey Early's Hotel" after a Charge Nurse who had worked there for a lifetime! There were a number of Nissen huts – those half-cylindrical corrugated steel shed buildings which stood about a hundred yards from the main hospital, and one of which housed the Occupational Therapy department. It had a large banner at one end with the printed message:

"Absence of occupation is not a rest. A mind quite vacant is a mind distressed."

Those words will remain forever in my mind, because they guided me during all my days in the hospital. One of the first things I was taught by Pat Hudson was to see the person first and then the illness. It was an excellent piece of advice that I remembered throughout my years at the Tyrone and Fermanagh Hospital. As a student, I had to attend regular lectures in the classrooms of the main building for courses on Psychiatry, Physiology and First Aid. At the same time in our own department, I also had to learn all the different craftworks practised by the patients – cane-work, rug-making, toy-making, embroidery, sewing, weaving, leatherwork and art. As part of my training I also had to watch a patient undergoing electro-convulsive therapy. This was supervised by qualified staff and the treatment was given to very depressed patients. I believe it was very successful.

As well as studying, meanwhile, I worked a five-day week beginning at 9am and finishing at 5pm with an hour for lunch. From 9am until 10.30am, we prepared work before going off to the different wards, alternating days between the male and female wards. In the afternoon, different groups of patients came to occupational therapy sessions in our own department. It was a full and varied schedule and all the stair-climbing was a physical challenge on my artificial limbs. Yet I knew from the very start that this is where I wanted to be, in what many would consider the forbidding environment of a huge psychiatric hospital facility, using the same tried and tested approach as generations before. I embarked happily on my life as a young working woman and, apart from that first day, I was treated as being as much "able-bodied" as any of my colleagues.

Chapter 11
Working girl

During meal times at the Tyrone and Fermanagh Hospital, there was always a very happy atmosphere in the staff canteen where the food would rank alongside any five-star restaurant today. Most people were happy to sit anywhere, but the Chief Executive Jimmy Short and the Matron sat at the same table every day. All the other staff including doctors and tradesmen intermingled. No one dared to occupy the seats chosen by Jimmy Short or the Matron. As the rest of us mixed when we ate lunch, I made a lot of friends from the very start. After eating, and for what remained of our lunch hour, a few of us played badminton in the Recreation Hall. Anna Gordon and I would team up to play Doreen Thompson and Mick O'Neill, the hospital's Entertainments Officer. Anna worked as a hairdresser for the patients and sometimes she would give me a wash and blow-dry – unofficially of course! Throughout the hospital there was a very friendly atmosphere. At first I thought that there were so many staff I would never get to know them all. But as the weeks went by, I was soon on familiar terms with everyone.

My mentor Pat Hodson lived in a caravan a short distance from my digs in the McCormicks' farmhouse. So most evenings after work in those early months, I would help Mrs McCormick with the washing-up and then cycle around to visit Pat. Her husband Frank was away all week working as a fitter in Ballymena. He came home on his motorbike at weekends when I would be down home in Fivemiletown. So during the week, Pat and I were glad of each other's company in the evenings in her compact but cosy caravan. She had all her meals in the hospital, so little or no cooking was done in the caravan, but she liked her independence and the caravan suited her lifestyle needs at the time. Even outside work, Pat spent hours teaching me as much as she knew about all the mental illnesses I would be dealing with in the hospital. She also gave me her own reference books to study. But it wasn't all work and on many of those long summer evenings, we cycled along the local roads enjoying the lovely countryside and we often visited the popular local beauty spot called "Lovers' Retreat" on the Camowen River, a short distance from the hospital grounds.

One night Pat loaned me her brand new "three-speed" bicycle to go to the cinema in Omagh. Bicycles like this were quite rare at the time, so of course I wanted to try it out going to and from the town. Anyway, when the film was over I discovered to my horror that Pat's bicycle was nowhere to be seen and I realized that it must have been stolen. In those days, there was no real need to lock bicycles, so I had simply left it leaning against the rails outside the cinema with all the other bikes. Now it was gone and how on earth was I to break the news to its proud owner? The next morning, I began by asking Pat, 'Have you ever had a bicycle stolen?' She knew immediately what I was trying to tell her. However, by good luck the bicycle was discovered a few days later in a hedge a few miles from the town. Much to my relief, it was still in good condition.

On many Wednesday and Friday afternoons, we arranged music and dance sessions for the patients in the Recreational Hall. We had an old wind-up gramophone with a lot of 78rpm records – "Circassian Circle", "Valeta Waltz", "Barn Dance" and so on. The patients really enjoyed these sessions. There was a piano in the hall and I would play it while the patients sang along. My music and art skills were already playing an important role in my work. I had an excellent grounding in art from Mother Teresa at the school. During the winter months of those early years in Omagh, I enrolled for night art classes at the Technical College, improving my knowledge and skills further.

On Thursday nights, I sometimes attended the films shown for patients at the Tyrone and Fermanagh Hospital by technician Armour Donnell. Often, however, some of the patients would become agitated and get up during the film to wander about in front of the screen. Someone would shout, 'Sit down or you'll be shot!' especially if a cowboy film was being shown! But the films had other value and the next day in our department, the patients would discuss the previous night's screening with strong opinions about who liked the film and who didn't. Some of the favourite film stars at the time were John Wayne, Elizabeth Taylor, Errol Flynn, Rock Hudson, Humphrey Bogart and James Stewart. Through those Friday discussions, the Hollywood stars all played vital roles in our therapy sessions.

We were paid on a monthly basis and when I received my first paycheque, I felt very confident and independent. After paying for my digs at McCormicks' and my meals in the hospital, I gave some money to my parents and I put the remainder into a Post Office savings account. I found that helpful in January, the most difficult month to make ends meet because most of us were paid before Christmas and had overspent.

Christmas was a very special time in the hospital, with decorations everywhere. Our O.T. department played a central role in this. During our therapy sessions, we made Yule Logs and cut out reindeers and Santas out of polystyrene which were then placed throughout the hospital. We also collected holly laurels and ivy, painted them white, and made them into Christmas arrangements. The patients really enjoyed this varied kind of work. A large Christmas

Party was always held in the Recreation Hall catering for a few hundred patients. They had mince pies, Christmas cake and some light refreshments. Of course Santa would arrive and hand out spot and novelty prizes. I recall one year during the festive season, I was working in the "A.A." unit where alcoholics and other substance abusers were treated. I sketched out a nativity scene and the patients painted it in. They were delighted with the end result and it was hung up in the staff canteen where everyone enjoyed it.

Another project I remember well from my first months in the Tyrone and Fermanagh Hospital was helping one of the patients to make herself a blouse, and with Pat's assistance, I helped to cut the fabric from an adapted pattern. The patient then sewed it by hand and week by week the blouse took shape, even if I had a few anxious moments over the work. Eventually, the day of the "fitting" arrived and I asked Pat to be there for that. The blouse actually turned out to be a good fit, except the collar didn't meet as the pattern meant it to. I rummaged around the department stocks until I came across a bow, which I then tied around the collar. It solved the problem: the patient was highly proud of the end result, and so was I.

From the start of my time at the Tyrone and Fermanagh Hospital, I became engrossed in learning all about different mental illnesses and I was intrigued by schizophrenia, manic depression, anxiety neurosis and so many more. I quickly found out that reading about an illness was altogether different from actually seeing it in a real patient. Under Pat Hudson's direction, I learned how to deal with the individual needs of patients and how to occupy them to the best of their ability. It amazed me how one particular woman stayed in a "catatonic" stupor for almost an entire year and then, on recovery, she could relate everything that I had said directly to her and even what I had said to others in her ward. Some patients were very obsessive, always having to sit on the same chair and in the same place in the O.T. department.

Others were in an agitated state and kept wandering about. I soon learned to take it all in my stride and eventually I became very confident in my work, finding it very easy to relate to the patients. I think the depressed patients were the most difficult to work with, but it was always very rewarding for me and the rest of the staff when they became well enough to go home.

The hospital grounds included plenty of good arable land, so a group of male patients who were mostly in the long-stay category and came from farming backgrounds, were involved in the day-to-day running of the hospital farm. This involved planting and harvesting crops which were used in the kitchens and there was a dairy herd which provided all the milk. It was very therapeutic work for those patients, and others who were involved under supervision in the upkeep of the grounds, including the wonderful flowerbeds. Female patients worked in the kitchen, the laundry and the sewing-room and also helped in cleaning the wards. All patients who worked were given pocket money allowances, but many of them were simply delighted to take part in growing vegetables and flowers which they could then sell for profit, mostly to staff. Then they could buy their own cigarettes, pipe tobacco and snuff, as well as having some sense of responsibility. When the weather was fine during the summer months, I would often take my groups of patients out for walks to admire the beautiful gardens and chat with the gardener and his workers.

Of course, one of the highlights of every summer back then was the annual train outing to the seaside resort of Bundoran in County Donegal. As many patients as possible went along, accompanied by several nurses. Firstly, most of these "holiday-makers" had to be kitted out with suitable clothing. Several large hampers of sandwiches and other picnic foods were taken along, and on arrival at Bundoran railway station, everyone had tea. Then before returning to Omagh, many of the male patients would have something a lot stronger. I believe the pubs in Bundoran had good takings on that day and it always took some time to get everyone gathered up for the return journey. Unfortunately, in the early 1960s, the Northern Ireland Railway services were discontinued for Omagh.

That was a big blow for more reasons than just missing the Bundoran outings. I always found the train a very convenient way to travel to the limb-fitting centre in Belfast. I could easily walk from the railway station in Great Victoria Street to Tyrone House in Ormeau Avenue and by then I could make my way around Belfast on foot. I loved especially going to Royal Avenue in the city centre where I could find the latest fashions in all the modern shops. It was during one of those train trips to Belfast around this time that I happened to come across an exhibition of paintings by the famous landscape artist Maurice C. Wilks. I admired his work and promised myself that if I ever had the time to paint again, it would be in his style. Most of the paintings in his exhibition were sold but in any event at the time, they were too expensive for me to purchase. I'm glad to say that, years later, I did become the proud owner of one of Wilks's works, which I bought from a local gallery.

Chapter 12

Girl about town

I remained in my digs at the McCormicks' for about a year. However, during the winter months I found it was quite a distance from Omagh, especially after a dance or a night out at the cinema. I felt sad leaving the McCormick family who had been so kind to me, but all my new friends were in Omagh town. I moved into Taggarts' of George's Street, a large three-storey house near the Sacred Heart Church and directly across the street from the INF ballroom. This meant I had further to cycle to my work in the hospital, almost two miles from the town centre.

While staying in Taggarts', I made great friends with Liz Duddy and Julia Taggart, a daughter in the house. Julia's own mother had died when she was a toddler. Julia's widowed father married again and she was then reared by her stepmother, my landlady, who had two younger children of her own. It was a hive of activity in Taggarts', with the extended family that also included Julia's older brothers, Jackie and Seamus, and her sister Sheila, me and several other boarders, a saddlery business on the ground floor and all the comings-and-goings of a busy town centre household. However, I felt quite at home there as I felt I already knew the family having admired Sheila Taggart's performances in the Town Hall pantos during those childhood trips. Jackie Taggart was a celebrated Tyrone Gaelic footballer around that time.

With the help of Julia and Liz, I learned to jive and dance in my new high-heel shoes. Because my social life was now pretty full, I had to have two pairs of artificial limbs, one set for the flat shoes which I wore to work, and the other for my leisure time. I remember well, bringing that first pair of high-heeled shoes up to Tyrone House in Belfast to have the new artificial feet shaped to their size and height. I was about nineteen years old at the time and I expected that some attempt would be made to discourage me from wearing high heels. Nothing was said, however, and I was delighted that the National Health Service, which had long since relieved my parents of the burden of paying for my artificial limbs, recognised that I just wanted to look, dress and act like all the young women of my age. My limb-fitter at the time understood this and he used to ask, 'What height is your latest boyfriend?' Other times it would be, 'What height would you like to be?' I suppose it is great to be able to choose your height. Once I had practised my walking and keeping my balance, which didn't take too long, I couldn't wait to go off dancing in my new high heels.

I soon mastered "Jiving" with my new limbs and shoes, so Julia, Liz and I could get dressed up in our finery and go off to dances. At that time there was a great choice of ballrooms. There was the INF across the street, the Star Ballroom, the Royal Arms and the Silver Birches, all in Omagh, with the "Gap" at Mullaslin, the Patrician Hall in Carrickmore and Clanabogan. Then further afield, there was the Astoria in Bundoran. We also went to the local cinema together and, after a night out at the cinema, we would call into Jack's Highland Café on George Street which served the best chips in Omagh. Sometimes our finances couldn't run to a plate of chips each, so we would buy one portion and divide it amongst the three of us.

I became a regular dance partner of Sean "Speedy" Hamilton who later became famous with The Plattermen Showband and he was one of the best known jivers about Omagh at the time. At first, Speedy didn't know about my artificial limbs. To keep my balance, I always had a strong grip on his hands. When he discovered the reason for this, he couldn't believe that I danced so well. But quite often at that time, my dance partners would not know about my artificial limbs and they often apologised for tramping on my toes, not knowing that I hadn't any! I just replied, 'It's OK, I never felt a thing.' I also remember that one night after a dance, a few friends and I got a lift home in a car. We all squeezed in and I had to sit on a man's knee. When he placed his hand on my knee, he became curious. I told him that I had a weak knee and had to wear a support for a few months!

One of the most popular venues for entertainment in the 1960s was the Royal Arms Hotel in Omagh. We were able to see and hear some of the top stars of that time, who were brought there by the owner Dai Watterson. I remember queuing up to hear Tom Jones, Acker Bilk, Dusty Springfield, Engelbert Humperdinck, The Bachelors and Jim Reeves. In those days there were no advance ticket sales; you just paid at the door. Local singer Frankie McBride, who was in the English charts at the time with "Five Little Fingers" drew huge crowds whenever he appeared. I remember that he drew the largest crowd ever to the Royal Arms one Boxing Night and I was among the dancers in that sensational crowd. This was during the Swinging Sixties and it was a great time to be alive and young and in Omagh. For us, it was also the Showband era with top acts such as, The Melody Aces, Clipper Carlton, Brian Coll, The Polka Dots coming from West Tyrone and the other big attractions such as The Miami, The Royal Showband and many others playing regularly at the local venues.

In the early 1960s one of the annual highlights was the summer carnival that took place in Omagh with dances in a marquee, erected in the Showgrounds on Sedan Avenue, right in the heart of the town. This meant we could dance to a different showband every night for a full week! Julie, Liz and I tried to go to as many of them as we could but our finances were often a bit thin and also it was important for me to get up in the morning, looking bright-eyed and ready for work at the Tyrone and Fermanagh Hospital.

After a busy week working in the hospital and those occasional dances and visits to the cinema, it was relaxing to go back home for the weekend and catch up on family life. It was my sister Una's task to leave a bicycle for me at McKeagney's Corner so that I could get off the bus in Fivemiletown and then cycle the short distance home. On one occasion, Una forgot to leave the bicycle for me. So after a week's work and with the additional walk home, my stumps were aching and I was totally exhausted. My mother gave Una a good scolding and she never forgot about the bicycle again!

As time went by, my tutor and friend Pat Hodson started to prepare for her return to England as her three-year contract with the Tyrone and Fermanagh Hospital was coming to an end. I knew I would miss Pat an awful lot; she had shown me so much kindness and had taught me all I knew. We held a "going away" party attended by staff as well as many of the patients who were also very sad to see her leave. As we were saying our goodbyes, Pat and I had a good laugh about the time I borrowed her new bike and had it stolen. We also recalled the morning when one of my artificial limbs suddenly broke as I was on my way to work. A metal rod connecting the leather straps to a knee joint had snapped. As a result of this, I was unable to walk or even move. Luckily a work colleague happened to be passing and saw my plight. He gave me a lift in his car to the nearest garage, Torney's on Omagh's Dublin Road, where a bemused mechanic welded the broken limb. I remember ringing the OT Department to explain why I was late for work: 'I'm here in the garage having my limb repaired.' I'm told some of the patients were very amused by this! After the welding was completed, I put on my repaired limb and continued on to my work.

Although my limb had been repaired shortly afterwards, I still had to attend the centre in Belfast to have a new pair made. These artificial limbs had to stand up to a lot of wear and tear as I wore them between twelve and fourteen hours most days even though they were not always comfortable. Very often I would have to make several trips to Tyrone House in Belfast before getting them right. Another problem I found was that during a spell of very hot weather, my stumps became very hot and sweaty. I asked a colleague, Staff Nurse Pat Conway, who worked in the woodwork department, if he would drill a few holes in my artificial limbs for ventilation purposes. At first he was reluctant to carry out my request but after some persuasion, he agreed. I found a vast improvement with that and I could feel my stumps were a lot cooler in the warm weather. However, during my next visit to the limb-fitting centre, I wondered what would be said about my "air-holes", but no comment was ever made.

On returning from Belfast, it was always nice to be greeted by my best friend Liz Duddy and we would then walk together down the "Rope Walk" – along the now disused railway line where Omagh's Great Northern Road is today – to her home. Her family background was very similar to my own. She had several brothers, one called John. Her dad, like my own, was called Barney and he would often make Liz and me and join in the family Rosary before going out for the evening. That was just like my own parents would have done at home.

Some weekends I didn't go home, especially if one of the popular dance bands were playing. One particular Friday night, the then famous Clipper Carlton Showband was playing at the Patrician Hall in Carrickmore. Gretta Woods, Claire Molloy and I headed off to the dance with our hair backcombed and held in place with loads of hairspray. With our make-up on we felt great and we danced the night away to popular tunes. Don Sheerin did his famous impression of Elvis Presley and he also sang "Juke Box Saturday Night" and many other hit favourites. At dances back then, only soft drinks were served. So when you were asked by your dance partner if you "wanted a lemonade", it was a good indication that he fancied you!

On the way home on the bus, I realised I had forgotten my door key. My landlady didn't like being woken at all hours of the morning, so it was agreed that I would stay in the Nurses' Home at the Tyrone and Fermanagh Hospital with Gretta and Claire. However, they didn't have a "pass" for that particular night, which meant we had to climb in through a small window which was usually left open for this purpose. Gretta climbed in first and it was decided that I should go next just in case I needed some help. 'I'll have to take one limb off or I'll never get through the window,' I called in to Gretta. I then tried to throw the artificial limb onto the bed inside, but instead it landed with a loud clatter on the floor. The noise roused the Home Warden, Miss Fenton, who came racing in to see what the commotion was. When she discovered my artificial limb, all she could do was laugh! I don't think I got Gretta and Claire into any trouble, and I don't believe my parents ever learned of this episode.

That same night, a few friends called in to chat with Gretta and Claire about the dance. These nurses then began to tell stories about other nights when they had had to sneak through the hospital grounds after hours, praying not to be caught by the night superintendant. Many a pair of good nylon stockings were torn while clambering over gates and fences and running through bushes and across lawns in an effort to get to the rooms. Sometimes the only means of escape was up a tree. On one occasion, little did the night superintendant realise that his very own daughter was up the tree looking down on him. In those days, the straight "pencil skirt" was the latest fashion but it was impossible to run or climb in. Anyone wearing one was advised that if they didn't want to be caught, they should take off their skirt and run. That night after the Clipper Carlton in Carrickmore, we talked and laughed about this well into the wee small hours.

Chapter 13

Changes at work and home

During the middle 1960s, the care of mentally ill patients began to change. Advances in medicine brought a greater understanding of psychiatric illnesses and care facilities were changed from the custodial "mental asylum" model to more open treatment centres. The appointment of a new Tyrone and Fermanagh Hospital consultant, Tom Haran, brought all of these changes to Omagh. The "closed ward" system was phased out, with the exception of a few wards that catered for very disturbed or unsettled patients. So most wards were opened up and the patients were allowed much more freedom to go out and about. Charge Nurse Willie Kyle, who had mainly worked in the woodwork department, was now appointed head of the Occupational Therapy department. Since I was still only 21 and needed guidance after my three years of regulated training, Willie helped me a lot in my professional development. He was a man of many skills and he set a high standard in all areas of his work, including monitoring time-keeping and the treatment of patients.

During all this change, a lot of the male patients were taken out of the closed wards and split into smaller working groups under the supervision of Joe Flanagan, Dermot Leonard and Mickey McCormick. These patients carried out manual tasks such as cutting hedges, mowing lawns and weeding gardens for staff members and other local people. Some also worked at bagging brewers grain at Watterson's Farm nearby and this was sold to local farmers as feed for their cattle. For the first time, those patients involved in this work were paid money, much to their delight. As a result, many were rehabilitated over time and became well enough to return home and lead normal lives. In the hospital itself, meanwhile, the "Kozy Corner" tuck shop was operated mainly by the female patients with only one member of staff involved. This gave initiative to these women and that was an important factor in their rehabilitation. There were some romances between patients of course, and the tuck shop was an ideal meeting place where they could have a cup of tea and a chat!

One of the highlights of the nursing year was "Prize-giving Day" with all the successful nurses receiving their certificates. This took place in the recreation hall, which was tastefully decorated with fresh cut flowers from the hospital garden. A lot of local dignitaries were invited to attend this function. I remember the nurses in their smart uniforms, waiting in rows in the hall to be called for their certificates. The "Chief Male Nurse's Cup" was awarded to the best student male nurse, while the "Matron's Cup" was awarded to the best female nurse. Photographs were published in the local newspapers. Some of these nurses went on to hold very prominent positions within their profession.

On our monthly payday, it was customary for someone to collect the pay cheques for a few friends and take them to a local bank where they would be cashed. On one occasion, I missed the chosen "banker", so I gave my cheque to a trustworthy patient, with the loan of my bike to speed him on his way to the bank to cash it for me. Then a few anxious hours passed with no sign of the patient, bike or money. I went to Staff Nurse Ben Wilkinson and told him of my plight. 'You did what?' he exclaimed and immediately burst out laughing, although I failed to see the joke at the time. Ben reassured me that he would locate the patient, bike and money because he had a good idea where he had gone. Sure enough, a short while later, Ben arrived back with the patient, my bike and the money intact but for the price of a few liquid refreshments!

Not everything came back, of course. A female patient was very fond of walking and she was given the job of walking the Matron's dog each day. The arrangement worked well for quite a while, until one day the patient arrived back with the dog lead but no dog. She was so engrossed in the walking, she hadn't even noticed the animal had slipped out and run away. She was one of our long stay patients at the time. We had some patients who remained in the hospital for as long as twenty to thirty years, so the staff got to know them very well. One particular male patient was impossible to beat at Draughts. I think both patients and staff throughout the hospital had tried to defeat him but to no avail. He was known by all simply as "The Champ".

Most of the craft work made in the department was bought by patients, staff and the general public. In all sale transactions, a receipt had to be written and money placed in a safe box, then on Friday morning the sales for the week were totalled. Sometimes there was a "discrepancy", perhaps two pence or six pence. It usually didn't amount to a lot, but we all dreaded the Friday morning "discrepancies". In all aspects of work, Charge Nurse Willie Kyle was very exact!

Every March, which was the last month of the financial year, we had to carry out stock-taking in the Occupational Therapy department. For this, we had to count everything, both in the main department and in the stores. This included all the rug wool, knitting wool, tapestry wool, spools, embroidery thread, lampshade material, leather, seating cord, dishcloth cotton, stool frames, canes, rug canvas, coat hangers and toy kits. This was one part of my work that I didn't like. When all was counted, the lists were audited by Bobby Jamieson and Jim

Henderson from the front office. We were always glad to get back to our normal routine.

But there were other breaks from the day-to-day activities that were enjoyable. During the summer, an Open Day was held within the hospital grounds for members of the public and it was always well supported by the local community and the families of staff members. This was a good way of fund-raising for the Patients' Comforts Fund. Lots of stalls were set up for the different items for sale, such as the cakes, homemade jams, bric-a-brac and lucky dip items. The patients' craftwork was also displayed for sale. Tickets were sold for the various activities and the "rickety wheel" was always a good money-spinner. Members of the public were given conducted tours around the hospital and these were popular, especially for retired staff. Eventually enough money was raised to purchase a holiday home for patients in Bundoran and a 27-seater bus which was used to transport the patients to and from the seaside resort for extended stays and also for day-trips. The holiday home was named "Fleming House" and Staff Nurse Cassie Kelly, who was also a marvellous cook, was assigned to run it for the season. Fleming House provided many of the patients with the first holiday they'd ever had. For staff on summer outings to Bundoran on their days off, Fleming House also was a great place to call in for some good bread and a cup of tea.

The bus used for these holidays and trips to and from Bundoran, meanwhile, was driven by Arthur McFarland. He always made sure that some of the most disturbed patients were placed in the seats at the front of the bus. There was a good reason for that, because it ensured that this was one bus the Customs officers didn't search. Just as well because I've heard that many cartons of cigarettes, packets of tobacco and other light contraband were often stashed under the back seat of the hospital bus!

Around the same time there were changes back at home too. Electricity had been installed on most farms and ours was among these. So there were no more Tilley lamps to be lit for illumination. Mammy even invested in a new electric cooker! All the farmyard sheds and the byre were also "lit up", making it a lot easier to feed the livestock and do the milking in winter. Soon Daddy had a new milking parlour built with an automated milking system installed.

Because I was in full-time employment, I was in a position to help my parents out financially. I also told my parents I was planning to take my two younger sisters to Bundoran for a few days on holiday. Most people did not go on family holidays back in those times but Mammy and Daddy thought it was a great idea and I knew Una and Madeline would love it. At the time, they were aged twelve and ten respectively and every weekend when I came home, they were waiting with bated breath to hear about my social life in Omagh. I had plenty of stories for them but I didn't let on that I was saving up to take them to Bundoran. Auntie Aggie was commissioned to knit a couple of cardigans for the girls.

Mammy bought them a couple of new dresses and she contributed some of her "egg money" as a spending allowance. I was paying for the accommodation at the Marine Hotel in the seaside resort's West End. I had originally planned for us to stay in a B&B but Mammy wanted to make sure we would have an evening meal arranged for each day, so I had to agree to the hotel. When I eventually told them that we were going to Bundoran for a few days at the beginning of August, Una and Madeline could barely contain their excitement.

'Don't forget to say your prayers at night,' Mammy called after us but I'm afraid it fell on deaf ears.

'Don't worry we'll be all right,' I replied, as we set off in the car with Uncle Jim who agreed to drive us all the way to Bundoran in his car. For the next few days we had a lovely time, although I had to budget carefully so that we didn't run out of money. Yet we did spend some time gambling on the slot machines, until we discovered for certain that they paid out less than we put in. We also went to the very popular Barbecue Café in the centre of the town where we treated ourselves to sausages and chips for a shilling followed by an ice-cream cone. The girls felt very grown up as this was their first time staying away from home and I'm sure our parents were delighted to see the three of us going off on a holiday together.

We spent a lot of time on the beach and while Madeline and Una paddled in the water, I took off my artificial limbs and paddled in the cool salt water along with them. It was so soothing on my warm stumps. Some passers-by stared at me in the paddling pool, but that was something I was getting used to over the years. I didn't mind so long as I was enjoying myself. The girls also found it enjoyable and it was something that we didn't have to pay for. We visited the other attractions near the beach, including the Museum Arcade and we were fascinated at the way that the Hall of Mirrors could transform our appearances, making us short and fat, tall and skinny, or with a small head on a big body. We joked and laughed for ages at the sight of ourselves in these mirrors.

One wet day during our holiday, I was wondering what we were going to do to pass the time. Then we spotted a poster in the hotel with the list of films being shown in the local cinema. It so happened that there was a matinée on that afternoon. I knew this would be a real treat for Una and Madeline because the small cinema in Fivemiletown had closed down some years before and they had not seen many films. The matinee show was a western starring John Wayne but we enjoyed it anyway.

We ate our last evening meal in the hotel on the Saturday knowing that the following morning, Uncle Jim was coming early to take us home. Then we sat at our bedroom window and watched the evening sun going down over the ocean. As we were going to bed that night, I said to my sisters, 'You can say a few prayers when you're in bed, so we'll not be telling a lie to Mammy when she asks.' Breakfast was a solemn affair the next morning as this was the end of our holiday. We were in no mood for going to Mass, but to miss Mass in those times would have been considered a grave sin. On our way to the chapel a few cyclists passed by and I wished I had my bicycle with me because it was so much easier on the limbs to get about. Later when we returned to the hotel, I said to Una and Madeline, 'Take a last walk along the beach and I'll pack our bags. Then I'll wait here just in case Uncle Jim comes early.'

I paid the hotel bill and sat on the bench at the front of the hotel. Eventually the girls returned with an ice-cream cone for each of us bought with the last of their "egg money". But the holiday wasn't over quite yet. When Uncle Jim arrived, he treated us to another visit to the Amusements at the beach and a big plate of chips, sausages and eggs in the Barbecue Café, during which he told us that our parents were missing us at home because the house was so quiet. On the way home, Una and Madeline talked endlessly about the wonderful time we'd had and I felt so proud to be able to give my mother even a few days breathing space.

On our arrival, Mammy was at the door waiting for us. We gave Theresa and Kevin, who at eight and four were the two youngest in the family, the sticks of Bundoran candy "rock" we had bought for them. We also gave Mammy and Daddy the gift we had chosen for them – a Holy Water font with "From Bundoran" printed across the front. I then set about packing my bag for my return to work in Omagh the following morning. As I did so, I was thinking that this short stay away from home might help my sisters to appreciate their comforts and not take them for granted.

Chapter 14

Losing my legs again

A new type of artificial limb was introduced in the early 1960s which did away with the "harness" made up of a belt around the waist with shoulder straps attached. The new limbs were strapped on above the knee and I was the first double amputee in Northern Ireland to be fitted with them. At the time my limb-fitter was Leslie Piper who took great care in taking the measurements, as well as making accurate casts of both my stumps. He said to me, 'Mary, you realise that this new type of limb will be a very big change and it will take you quite a while to get used to them.'

His words resounded in my ears as I left the limb-fitting centre that day. For twenty years, I had been wearing the same type of limbs with the straps and belt attached and they seemed to be part of my natural body. In my day-to-day life, I had adjusted to them, almost as much as anyone else has adjusted to their own legs. Now here again, I was about to lose the only legs I had ever known and then I would have to adapt my life to wearing new artificial limbs, that would feel strange and uncomfortable, at least for the initial period. These thoughts played around in my mind as I waited for the day when I would try on the new artificial limbs.

A few months later, that day came and Mr Piper helped me to strap them on. At first it just felt odd not having the belt around my waist. Then, as I stood up, I realised to my horror that I was unable to take even a single step. I knew then I would have to learn to walk all over again. I was very disappointed, because while I had been apprehensive about losing my old limbs, I also had such high hopes of what the new ones might allow me to do. Finally, with the help of Mr Piper, I took a few faltering steps. I rested and then tried again, hour after hour, trying to master the new limbs that would have to serve as my legs and allow me to resume my life with all the activity that was involved in it. Finally, after a few tiring hours, I was able to keep my balance and walk unaided on the new legs. Even so, I was very relieved to put my old limbs back on again with all their belts and buckles.

The old limbs were made of tin and leather by an English company called Hanger. Their official name was "No. 8 Metal". The new limbs were also made in England by Hanger but apart from the new fastening methods, they were composed of titanium from the knee to the ankle where they slotted into the artificial foot. While titanium was the new wonder element in medical prosthetics because of its low density, it wasn't really much lighter in artificial limbs.

I had to return to the limb-fitting centre for several further appointments during which I spent hours each time learning to walk on my new limbs. Mr Piper was always there to encourage and compliment me on how well I was doing. At that time, physiotherapists were not involved in rehabilitation for amputees and I don't recall any physiotherapy before the mid-1970s. Instead, the work was left to non-medical but high skilled technicians like the wonderful Mr Piper, who was really my sole point of contact for limb-fitting over a period of about twenty years. Eventually the day arrived when I was allowed to take my new limbs home to wear, although it would be quite some time before I could adapt myself to using them for a complete day. I had to compromise – I wore my old limbs to work and then changed into my new limbs in the evening.

For the first few months, I found that my new limbs were quite tiring. I came to realise that I was missing the support of the thigh leather corset and the external hinges on either side of the knees which all helped to bear some of the weight pressure on my leg stumps. After walking a very short distance in the new limbs, I found my stumps were almost numb and I began to suffer a lot of pressure sores. Mr Piper's words were borne out; these limbs were a big change, but I just had to grin and bear it. Meanwhile, my friends and my colleagues at work thought the new limbs were a big change for the better, although my new boyfriend John, who later became my husband, understood more than anyone the drastic change I was going through in trying to adjust to these new limbs.

Over time, of course, I did get used to them and I found them much easier to put on and take off because I no longer had to deal with the belt around my waist or the shoulder straps. My thigh muscles were also able to develop to their normal size, because before this they were constricted with each encased in a leather corset. During the period of adjusting to the new limbs, which took about twelve months in all, I had great support from my work colleagues in the hospital and I could sit whenever I found it hard going. When I became more accustomed to my limbs, I also appreciated their added value in features that allowed them to appear more like natural legs. For instance, they had a soft silicone covering in a colour and tone that resembled human skin. This was some compensation for all of the pain and frustration of wearing them.

My parents and the rest of my family were keen to see my new limbs. My mother always asked, 'Are they comfortable?' To put her mind at ease I usually told her that they were. In actual fact, this was not always the case and several alterations had to be made before I could honestly answer without reservation that they were comfortable.

Apart from the initial discomfort and pain of adjusting to the new limbs, there were other drawbacks. For a start, I found it more difficult to ride my bicycle with the new limbs. So I found more convenient accommodation. This time, I moved to Jim Aiken's house in Starrs Crescent in the Gallows Hill district of Omagh town. Jim also worked at the hospital so he was able to give me a lift to work. However, this meant I had to be up an hour earlier because Jim started at 8am while I didn't have to be in until 9am. A lot of mornings, especially during the dark winter months, I wasn't up in time. This meant I had to walk a distance of about half a mile to the Dublin Road, where I got a lift with another colleague, Arthur McFarland. On some of those mornings, a neighbour called Sammy Johnston, who lived opposite the Aikens, would accompany me on the walk through the town. We would have to help each other down Gallows Hill because Sammy would often have been "out on the town" the night before. On those occasions, it was hard to tell who was helping who!

My transport problem was short-lived, however, because around this time the NHS informed me that I was eligible for one of the three-wheeled vehicles that were officially called the "Thundersley Invacar". It was made of fibreglass and had a two-stroke engine. Apart from the missing wheel in its design, the main feature of this car was that there were no foot pedals or steering wheel. It was completely controlled by hand using levers that were like motorbike handles. To apply the brakes, you pushed down on the handles. It more than suited my needs, even if it only had one seat for the driver and the fibreglass body provided little protection against the elements. This small car was fully automatic, so after a few lessons with a local garage man, Tony McCann, I was capable of driving to work. Also there was no fuel gauge on the dashboard, so I had to remember to "top up" the petrol tank every so often. Just in case I ran out, I learned to carry a can of petrol at all times.

Within a few months, I had passed my driving test and I was on the road to complete independence. It was small enough to tuck into the smallest space, so I did not need a special parking spot at work; which is just as well because this was long before "blue badge" parking became the norm. While others might have pointed and stared as I trundled along in my little "three-wheeler", my family and friends also took this little car to their hearts. And, like the famous car in which Donald Campbell set the world speed records around that time, my three-wheeler was also known as "Bluebird" on account of its bright blue colour!

Chapter 15

Love and Marriage

I was off work and home for the Easter holiday weekend when I decided to go with a few of my friends to a dance in Augher Parish Hall on the Sunday night. The Patsy Farrell Band from Ballygawley was playing that night. John O'Brien was the drummer and had been with the band for a few years at theat time. I had often seen him at the local dances and he wasn't a complete stranger because he sometimes danced with me. During the interval when the band took a break that night in Augher, John came over to talk to me and he asked if he could leave me home after the dance. I agreed of course, and this was the start of our romance.

As the weeks and months went by, John and I discovered that we had a lot of interests in common. The main one, of course, was music and dancing. He was a fine musician and a multi-instrumentalist. Apart from playing in Patsy Farrell's dance bands, he was a member of the Noel Hackett Ceilidh Band and the Pride of Erin Ceilidh Band, as well as the St Lawrence's Pipe Band from Fintona. He also had a full-time day job as a lorry driver with J.J. Scallon, which was at that time, a big public works company based in Irvinestown and involved in major road developments and other work throughout the North.

John and I enjoyed each other's company so much that we began to spend more and more time together. John had grown up as an only child and now he was living with his widowed father Frank. He was great fun to be with and he seemed to have a lot of friends. I quickly discovered that he had the kind of engaging personality that made friends easily wherever he went. My own family grew very fond of him and our relationship blossomed. Soon we were both keen to settle down and spend the rest of our lives together and so we got engaged on my twenty-fifth birthday in June. We set the wedding date for Saturday 1 October 1966, which was the following year.

Our parents were delighted for us. As the days and weeks passed, all I could think of was my wedding day and how many preparations had to be done. We booked the hotel and, as the wedding drew nearer, we checked out that the menu and everything else was in order. Meanwhile, I spotted a wedding dress I liked in the window of a draper's shop in Omagh. The next day after work, I went into the shop to try it on and, to my delight, it was a perfect fit. Month by month as I received my pay cheques, I paid for the dress. I also bought some blue material for my mother to make a bridesmaid's dress for my sister Madeline. As all this was going on, John and I compiled a list of wedding guests, including family, relatives, friends and neighbours on both sides. John asked his best friend Liam McFarland to be the best man. Liam was also a close neighbour from the next townland and both he and John were in the Fintona pipe band where Liam played bagpipes and John played drums.

The excitement over the wedding grew, even among the patients in my department who kept reminding me how many days were left until 1 October. And before the big day, the patients and staff in the O.T. department held a little celebration party and presented me with a wedding present.

My perfect day eventually arrived and we were blessed with beautiful autumn weather. My brother John was home from London with his new wife Briege, who was originally from Belmullet in

County Mayo. I had attended their wedding some time before when I went over to the London ceremony with our parents and my brother Brian. That had been a wonderful family reunion for both the Tyrone and Mayo families. For my wedding, John brought along his new camera and he took lots of family photographs. As I left the house with my father, my heart was full of mixed emotions – some sad, some happy, some proud, and some excited. I realised I was now beginning a new era in my life. I was about to become a married woman with a husband to share the rest of my life.

For the Nuptial Mass in our local chapel, my Aunt Kitty was the organist and Daddy was the soloist, while my youngest brother Kevin was one of the altar boys. As my father sang "Ave Maria" and "Panis Angelicus", I could feel my eyes fill with tears. It must have been a poignant moment for my parents also. Looking back to the day of my horrific accident twenty-two years earlier, I am sure they must have wondered if this day would ever come.

At the reception in a local hotel afterwards, it was wonderful to see members of both our families enjoying themselves together. I sang a song, "This is my Lovely Day", accompanied by Patsy Farrell on the accordion and my Aunt Kitty on the piano who then continued to provide the musical entertainment. It was not the norm at that time for bands to play at weddings, much less have a DJ late into the night. Yet there was no shortage of real musical talent there on our wedding day and we had a steady procession of guests coming up to do their turn. But the celebration passed far too quickly and, reluctantly, I had to change out of my wedding dress and into my going-away outfit and we set off from Fivemiletown. For the next five days, we toured around Ireland taking in places of interest such as Glendalough, the Vale of Avoca in Wicklow and, of course, Dublin city. There was plenty to take in but, in the end, we were both glad to get back to our jobs and a normal routine.

As a young married couple, we stayed at first with John's father Frank, who had been a widower for the past three years. His country cottage outside Dromore had no modern facilities, not even running water or electricity. Nevertheless John and I were very content because we both knew it was just a start in our life together. Living with John's father gave us a chance to start saving some money with a view to purchasing a home of our own one day. Meanwhile, a good friend from Fintona, Patsy McCann, installed a gas cooker and gas lighting in the cottage, which was a big help. However, the only heating we had in the cottage was an open-hearth fire. With no water on tap, I was glad to have the launderette in Omagh, ten miles away, to wash and dry the clothes, especially during the winter months.

With no electricity, of course, we couldn't have a TV and so we had to make do with a battery radio. Looking back, this proved no hardship for us and during the long winter evenings we were happy to provide our own entertainment. We purchased an acoustic guitar and a music book showing the chords. We then spent our nights teaching each other to play the guitar. I had studied the theory of music and had passed several exams in both violin and piano; John had a natural musical ability. He could already play the accordion, violin, drums and harmonica. This meant that he could pick up the guitar chords more quickly than me. However, John's father had many a laugh at our expense before we became proficient enough to play that guitar properly. Eventually, I could accompany John on rhythm guitar when he played the accordion or violin. Our cosy romantic duo then grew and multiplied with my father-in-law Frank on the fiddle, John and a local neighbour, Willie Crawford, both on accordion, our "gas fitter" friend, Patsy McCann, on banjo, and Martin Cunningham and myself on guitar. While other households huddled in front of the TV, we had many an enjoyable night's music through those winter months. However, being the only woman in a house full of men back then, meant that I was expected to make the tea. Many a pot was brewed to accompany plates of sandwiches made with my homemade soda bread. I should have been exhausted, but I always seemed to have bundles of energy for those wonderful musical winter evenings we shared.

During that time of year, of course, charity fund-raising functions were held throughout Dromore parish involving dances, concerts and guest teas. For one of these concerts, some featured artists failed to arrive. The Master of Ceremonies for the night was Noel Hackett from the ceilidh band in which John played the drums. Noel asked John and me to step into the breach and perform. I only knew two entire songs at that time, "The Boys from the County Armagh" and "The Rose of Arranmore". We performed these and the audience applause warranted another song but I couldn't oblige because I didn't know any more. John, on the other hand, had quite a selection of songs that he could deliver, and I resolved that night to learn more for such occasions. So we bought a battery operated tape player and from this we learned most of our songs. It was a reel-to-reel battery operated tape-recorder that we still have as a keepsake and we used it to record songs from the radio in our kitchen. John's first choice was traditional Irish music but I preferred American Country music. So while I carried out my housework, I listened to tapes of Jean Shepard, Lorreta Lynn, Kitty Wells and Patsy Cline, singing along until I had the words and melodies thoroughly memorised. After this, we were in demand for other fund-raising functions and our popularity grew.

Our entry onto the entertainment stage coincided with the arrival of the lounge bar scene in local towns and villages. It wasn't long until we were approached by some of these bar owners and asked to entertain their customers, mostly at the weekends. The Market Bar in Omagh, owned by Dan McGettigan, was our first venue back about the start of 1967. In the beginning, I was nervous about performing in public before an audience I didn't really know. John was quite at ease, however, having been used to dance band performances all over the region. As the weeks and months went by, I became more confident. Our repertoire included Irish ballads, Country and Western, traditional music and our trademark speciality was singing duets. We soon became well known on the lounge bar entertainment circuit simply as "John and Mary".

We both had to keep on our day jobs, of course, and travelling to work in "Bluebird" during those winter months was quite daunting, especially if there was ice or snow. Then the ten miles distance from Dromore seemed a lot longer. The heating system in that small car was totally inadequate, so I had to wear layers of warm clothes in a bid to stay warm as I drove along the narrow country roads in freezing temperatures. But it was lovely to come home from a day's work to find a blazing fire in the grate, stoked up by John's father to welcome us home. My new husband and I were both glad to be off work during the Christmas holidays, not least because we had a lot of functions to play at, mostly Christmas Draws!

Meanwhile, my "culinary skills" were improving and I was delighted when my first Christmas dinner turned out to be a success. Later on, in the evening, we drove up to Fivemiletown to see my family.

Chapter 16
New best friend and family

Staff Nurse Bella Evans was sent to work with me in the Arts and Crafts department in 1966. From day one we became great workmates, as well as lifelong friends. By that time, my best friend Liz Duddy had moved away from Omagh having got married in September 1961. She lived in England for a while but had been unable to come over for my wedding because she was pregnant at the time. Some years later, Liz and her husband emigrated to Australia where she remains to this day, although we keep in touch regularly.

When she came into the department at the Tyrone and Fermanagh Hospital, Bella was just recently married, so we that in common as well as our work. She was also light-hearted with an outgoing personality like myself and we both had a great rapport with the patients. We were really a great team, seeming to know instinctively how to support each other and do the best for all the patients in our care. Very often the Matron or Assistant Matron would call by. On one particular day, the Matron commented on the lovely atmosphere in our department. The patients were listening to a tape of well-known ballads which I had brought in for their enjoyment and some of the other patients were singing along to it.

So things were running along smoothly at work when, after a few mornings of being sick and a visit to my family doctor, it was confirmed that I was pregnant with our first child. My parents and John's father were thrilled with the news, because this would be the first grandchild in both families. Then a few weeks later, Bella revealed her own good news – she was pregnant also. When the patients heard, they laughed and said it must be contagious!

As the weeks and months went by, Bella and I knew that it was only a matter of time until we would both be off on maternity leave. Robert McKinley, who was in charge of salaries and wages, informed us that an 18-week maternity leave had been introduced. We would be the first members of staff to avail of this new regulation and it meant that we would retain our continuous service with no loss of conditions or salary when we returned to work. But there would be changes in my condition, nonetheless, because in January 1968 – just one month before my due date for our first child – we moved to a new home which was better known as the "Chapel House" in Dromore.

John's father had been appointed Sexton and caretaker of St Dympna's Church, and the two-storey house that came with the job was situated on the outskirts of the village, about a quarter of a mile from the village itself. His duties included opening and closing the church doors, ringing the bell for the Angelus and other church events, as well as taking care of the vestments, the Sacristy and other parts of the church, along with maintaining the grounds. The new house had all the modern amenities, as well as a large garden to the front and back. We now had electricity, so we bought our first TV, a washing machine and a record player. There was a solid-fuel cooker in the kitchen, which supplied both heat and hot water. The sheer comfort in which we now found ourselves was a sharp contrast to the small country cottage where we had lived for the past two years.

Some things remained the same however, and our new home became another house of music. Indeed, our parish curate in Dromore, the renowned local historian and credit union pioneer, Father Paddy

Gallagher, regularly called into the "Chapel House" where he enjoyed listening to us practising our music at night. He lived just a short distance away. Meanwhile, my father-in-law Frank was very happy in his new job and all its varied duties inside and outside the church. He also found time for his favourite hobby – gardening – and in the back garden of the house, he was soon growing a plentiful supply of wonderful vegetables. Meanwhile, I was kept very busy inside our new home, hanging curtains, choosing floor coverings and arranging furniture for all the rooms. My younger sister Teresa was now a student nurse at the Tyrone County Hospital in Omagh and on her days off she came along to give me a helping hand. My maternity leave had started and after working constantly for ten years at the Tyrone and Fermanagh Hospital, it felt odd to be off for a long stretch.

During those last few months before the birth, I had found that the extra weight I was carrying put a lot of pressure on my stumps. Both my father-in-law and John were very understanding and they helped out with the household chores as much as they could. I wasn't idle however, and in my spare time I knitted little matinee coats, bonnets and more for our new arrival. I just knew that everything would work out.

Then one Friday morning, I awoke with what I took to be my first labour pains. I got up, put on my limbs and went about my normal household duties, including cooking the breakfast. Later on in the evening, the pains returned with a vengeance, so John drove me to the General Hospital in Omagh, where I was admitted to the Maternity Ward. After undressing and taking off my limbs, I was put into bed. I had previously heard that a first baby can take quite a while to arrive, but I had never imagined that after twenty hours I would still be in labour. So I was then transferred by ambulance to the Tyrone County Hospital, also in Omagh. I remember asking the nurse who was accompanying me to make sure that my limbs were in the ambulance.

After home confinements were discontinued in the late 1950s, expectant mothers were admitted to the "lying in" facilities at Omagh General Hospital on Woodside Avenue. Here midwives took care of the deliveries with the help of doctors if needed. However, if any complications arose, the mothers were transferred to the Tyrone County Hospital about half a mile away where gynaecologists were on duty. After I was taken to the County, I was examined by Surgeon Patterson who told me that I would have to have a forceps delivery. He then advised me to be perfectly still; otherwise my baby could be harmed. On hearing this, I lay as still as a log. After some time, which seemed like hours to me, I was finally relieved to hear the cry of our first-born – a beautiful baby boy who weighed in at a hefty 9lbs. I still remember vividly that while a junior doctor and a nurse were inserting stitches, they discussed the latest type of cars on the market, just as if they were chatting in the canteen!

I was exhausted, but happy at the same time that it was "all over". Sister McGarvey, who was in charge, approached me as I was being wheeled to the ward to enquire if I would prefer to be in a single room on account of my limbs. I replied that I would much rather be in the open ward. As I was being helped into bed, I had to check again that my limbs were there beside me, knowing that if they were misplaced, they might just disappear in such a big hospital. A nurse had placed them into a black bag to carry them and I was afraid they would be mistaken for rubbish and sent out to the bins!

When I was settled, John was allowed into the ward to see us for a few minutes and, like all new fathers, he was beaming with pride. Together we gazed at our new son who was now fast asleep in the Perspex crib. After a welcome cup of tea and toast, I drifted into a well-earned sleep, but before doing so I repeated the date over and over in my head to commit it to memory. Saturday 25 February 1968, how could I ever forget?

The next day was Sunday, so I had lots of visitors. The proud daddy John was the first to arrive, followed by my parents who were very keen to meet their first grandchild. When all the visitors left, all the new mothers in the ward got chatting about the different kind of births we had experienced. Then later on when the night staff came on duty, one of the nurses recognised me as an entertainer, so I had to sing a few songs for everyone! The following days were spent feeding, changing and cleaning our new little bundles of joy. Finally when the day came for us to go home, a staff nurse called after me, 'See you next year!'

I replied, 'Not if I can help it!'

Coming from a large family as the oldest girl, I grew up looking after my younger brothers and sisters. So it wasn't long before I got into a routine with my own new baby we had christened Aidan. At that time, there was no such thing as "disposable" nappies, only the terry-towelling ones that had to be washed, dried and reused. So with so much extra laundry to do, I was glad of our new washing machine. My parents had given us a present of a Moses basket, which I placed on the floor at the side of our bed. During the night when my limbs were off, this enabled me to lift Aidan out to feed and change him. John and I usually took turns at bottle-feeding and changing the baby.

In the immediate weeks following the birth, I had lost a lot of body weight, which meant that my limbs were not fitting me properly. I had to wear extra "stump socks" to compensate for this loss of weight and to allow me to wear the limbs more comfortably. Yet no matter what I did, for the first time in my life I suffered excessive pain in the bottom of both my stumps. However, as the days and weeks went by, I regained my normal weight and the pain gradually subsided. I was glad to have my youngest sister, Teresa, to help me out at that time.

Meanwhile, I had heard from Bella that she had a little baby girl who was christened Sharon. Like myself, Bella was looking for a childminder at that time because we were both scheduled to return to work in six weeks. My mother volunteered to look after Aidan, but she lived too far away and she had already reared seven children of her own. I thought she had done enough childminding! Then one day, while out walking and pushing the pram, I just happened to meet a very pleasant woman. We got talking and I explained to her that I was hoping to return to work and so I was looking for someone to mind the baby. She said that she would be very interested, but she would have to think about it and let me know. A few days later, she called to the house to say she would take the job. Her name was Mary Anne Harper, but we all came to call her "Gran". Her own family was all grown up and she enjoyed looking after children, she told me. I told John and Frank about "Gran" and they both knew her; so they were delighted with the news.

Before finally returning to work, I had to visit the limb-fitting centre in Belfast. My weight had now stabilized, so I was to be fitted for a new pair of limbs. John drove me to Belfast and I thought that our absence for this would be a good time for Aidan and "Gran" to get acquainted. We arrived home to find Aidan very content and sound asleep.

Bella and I both returned to work about mid-April. Although Aidan was in good hands, I still felt a pang of guilt leaving him. However, we were still very busy in the O.T. department. A lot of new patients had arrived, but the long-stay patients were delighted to see us back. Then on arriving home from that first day back at work, I found out that "Gran" was not only a childminder but a housekeeper as well. She had the house cleaned from top to bottom and the laundry done. I then realised just how lucky I was.

My parting words to the staff nurse in the Maternity Ward who had told me she would see me next year, came back to haunt me. For the following year, on 10 October 1969, Sean, our second son was born. This time I had a straightforward delivery with no complications. At the time, it was the general practice for mothers to stay in the hospital for seven days after the birth of their baby. But I was missing Aidan who was only sixteen months old at that stage, so I pleaded with Surgeon Patterson and he allowed me to go home in a few days. Aidan even came to the hospital with his daddy to take me home with his new brother Sean. John and Frank were delighted to have me and our new baby home and we were all very proud of our two sons. Gran was delighted too, and she immediately took to calling Aidan and Sean "my boys". She was such a loving and devoted childminder and she came to the "Chapel House" every morning on Jim Garrity's milk float. I would watch out for the arrival of the milk and the minder, satisfied the boys were in safe hands, I would then head off for work in Omagh. When I got home, and John was there to look after Aidan and Sean, I would then take Gran to her own home in "Bluebird". That usually meant taking her grandchildren, Gerald and Siobhán Hackett, off for a little ride.

When I returned to work after my second 18 weeks maternity leave, I found that the department had now been moved from the Nissan hut to a more modern building known as Hilltop. It was much brighter and roomier and the nurses' home was situated close by so, during our lunch break, Bella and I often visited Miss Fenton, the Home Warden. She always had a good laugh about the night I climbed through the window!

My life was now busier than ever. When Sean was only four weeks old, I had to play at a wedding, as John was unable to find a replacement musician. I felt guilty leaving the boys but knew they were in good hands with "Gran". I was into my second ten years of working in the hospital and I was still leading a very busy life – a mother of two young sons, an entertainer and also in full-time employment as an assistant occupational therapist. How could I possibly handle any more?

Distressing Fivemiletown Affair

CHILD LOSES LEGS

A distressing accident occurred during harvesting operations on Wednesday evening of last week, when a child aged two years, daughter of Bernard McMahon, Breakley, Fivemiletown, had both legs severed.

It appears the child crept into the corn and became entangled in the reaper. The child was immediately removed to Fermanagh County Hospital, where its condition is still regarded as rather critical.

Part of the article in the local press at the time.

Fivemiletown street in the 1950s.

Only photo of myself prior
to the accident.

My new bicycle.

Una (wearing wellingtons that my mother had adapted for me!) and myself.

Me at the beach.

Granny, Keenan, my mother, and me.

Jimmy McKeshlan,
Kitchie Robinson
with me, Una and
Madeline on the
farm.

Myself and Miss Phelps
in Trafalgar Square
feeding the pigeons —
1953.

Myself, Eileen McMahon, Una and Theresa getting ready for the weekly dance.

Madeline and myself on holiday in Bundoran.

Playing tennis.

Myself in a new dress.

Pat Hudson and myself when I started work at the Tryone and Fermanagh Hospital in Omagh (1958).

The McMahon family with Mum and Dad.

John and myself on our wedding day (1966).

Below: Our childminder Gran with Aidan as a baby.

Myself, John and Aidan.

Below: Our family on Sean's confirmation day.

Bluebird.

Below: John and Mary
 – two-piece band.

Myself and Joe Burke and son Sean.

Prince Charles during a visit to Omagh after the 1998 bomb. He visited the
Monday Art Group in Omagh Youth Centre.

Willie McCarter and myself with paintings for exhibition

Myself tutoring local artist group at a weekly class.

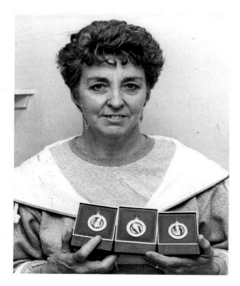

Winning three gold medals at
the National Amputee Games
in 1990.

In Jersey.

With Una in Boston.

With Boston Commissioner of Police, Mick Roache. I was awarded an honorary member of the Boston Police (1991).

Below. The Omagh Phab group at the biggest disabled conference ever held worldwide in Moscow (1992).

In a KGB hat in Moscow.

Below. Local artist Jean Gregory, Liam Breen, and myself at an art exhibition in Paris, 2007.

Bobby Charlton, myself and Nigel Hawthorn at
The Mansion House, London, 1999.

Tessa Sanderson, myself and Shirley Bassey at The Mansion House.

Nick Owen and myself at the Mansion House, London.

Richard Attenborough and myself at the Mansion House, London.

Above: Myself and Mary McAleese (then the President of Ireland) during a visit to Omagh.

Left: Margo O'Donnell and myself.

Daniel O'Donnell and myself.

Below: Dr Roger Parke (consultant at Musgrave Park Hospital).

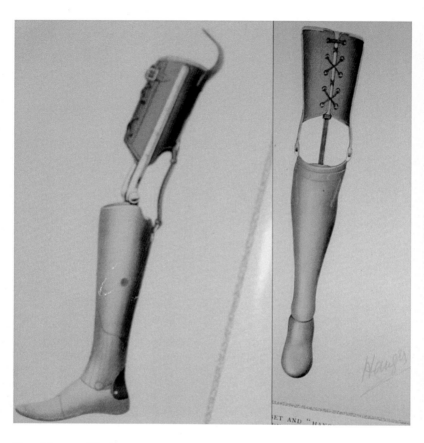

The old type of limbs.

My current limbs.

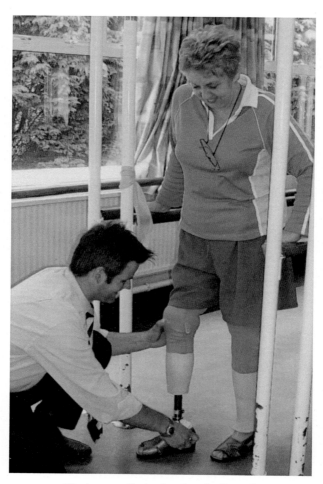

Having new limbs fitted and adjusted

Me receiving an MBE for Services to Disabled, 2000.

My gorgeous grandchildren: Sarah, Rory, Joanne, Clare, Jessica
Niamh, and Hannah.

Chapter 17

Not a leg between us

After the closure in 1965 of the Great Northern Railway line through Omagh to Derry, John often had to drive me up to Belfast for my appointments. So he was no stranger to the limb-fitting centre, which was now situated at the Musgrave Park Hospital in Belfast. The new facility was on the outskirts of the city and it was more clinic-orientated than Tyrone House and had more spacious rooms. At Musgrave Park, I could see recent amputees trying to walk on their new limbs with the help of physiotherapists who had started to take over that role from the technicians like my Mr Piper. I really felt for the older patients who were trying to walk and I realised that since I could barely remember my first experience of artificial limbs, this major adjustment had almost come naturally to me.

Yet with my own busy life, my limbs now had to stand up to a lot of wear and tear which meant I regularly had to go to Belfast to have new knee straps attached, or to have feet repaired and even for a new supply of "stump socks". Occasionally I was requested to talk to patients who were about to have their limbs amputated. The request usually came from Musgrave Park Hospital through Mr Roger Parke, who would approach me when I was in for an appointment of my own. I tried to put their mind at ease by explaining that you could still live a full and rewarding life, citing myself as an example. Down through the years I have kept in touch with many of the people that I spoke to back then and they are all doing fine.

Quite a few years ago I was then asked to visit Carty McGirr, a young man from Trillick, County Tyrone, who had lost both his legs in a farming accident when his legs got caught in the shaft of a slurry tanker. Just like me, he lost both legs, one above the knee and the other below. He was lucky that a sixteen-year-old boy witnessed the accident and raised the alarm. Otherwise, Carty would certainly have bled to death in that field at only thirty-nine years of age. He was rushed to hospital in Enniskillen where he spent nine hours in the operating theatre. Then after seven weeks in hospital, he returned home in a wheelchair. It was really only then that the shock set in and, among other symptoms, he could not bear to sit in a car being driven at more than 30 miles per hour.

Carty was told that he would eventually have to be fitted with a pair of artificial limbs, but this did nothing to relieve his deep depression brought on by the shock. At that point, I was asked to have a word with him. I can still remember vividly walking up the corridor into the ward to meet Carty who was quite surprised when he was told that I was walking on a pair of artificial limbs. Naturally, he had a lot of questions – how the limbs were made and fitted and so on. I knew then from Carty's attitude that he was determined to deal with any challenges that lay ahead.

It was natural that we bonded so closely from the outset. We were both from Tyrone and from similar rural farming backgrounds and we now shared this challenge of leading a full and active life with artificial limbs. As we were saying our goodbyes, I said, "When you get your new legs we will dance together". He promised me that we would. Three months later, he was fitted for artificial limbs and with the support of his wife and family, along with his good neighbours, Carty more than rose to the challenge and he resumed farming again.

As fairly close neighbours, we became firm friends. I encouraged him to learn to swim and he has never looked back. We even spend a lot of time comparing new artificial limbs. As for that first day promise in the hospital, a few years later at his own daughter's wedding reception, Carty and I had our first dance together, and not a leg between us!

During the early years of the Troubles in Northern Ireland, I was asked to visit two young women in Belfast who had both lost limbs as a result of a bomb explosion. As John and I travelled up to see them, I found myself dwelling on the fact that in the space of minutes their lives had been changed drastically when they both became amputees for the rest of their lives. I tried to find the right words of comfort and encouragement and to tell them that it is possible to still live a full life, even with artificial limbs. As usual, I cited myself as an example. But they were so different from me. I had never known, nor remembered, my real legs and only knew life with artificial limbs. On meeting these young bomb victims, I learned that one of them was out shopping for her wedding dress when she got caught up in the explosion. The anticipated happiest time of her life when she would marry her fiancé from Donegal had been turned into a horrific tragedy by an indiscriminate bomb in a public place while people were going about their day-to-day lives. There were 130 people in the Abercorn Bar in central Belfast that Saturday afternoon, when one young woman was killed in what the Belfast City Coroner described as "pathological murder". Everyone else was injured, some dreadfully. Of the two sisters I met, one had lost both legs, an arm and an eye in the blast; her sister had also lost both legs. It seemed such a terrible waste. Knowing the struggles that lay ahead of these two young women who would have to adapt to a new and very challenging way of life, I came away with a prayer that they would be able to surmount the obstacles that would be in their paths. I knew from experience that there would be many of them.

As the dreadful toll of conflict rose during those dark years of the Troubles, I often reflected on those who were killed in the succession of outrages, on those who were injured and on those maimed dreadfully in body and soul. As in my own case, the actual circumstances of the tragedy are often not discussed with the victim who usually is unable to remember precisely what happened to them. Sadly, the desire to spare sensitive feelings can have the opposite effect. However, I am probably as guilty as everyone else in this regard, because I don't know what became of the two girls I met, after their lives were ripped apart in the Abercorn on that Saturday afternoon in the spring of 1972.

Helping people to cope with trauma and other challenges in life was part and parcel of my professional life, of course, but often my efforts had to extend beyond the normal nine-to-five schedule. The Matron knew about my experience in the entertainment world and one day she asked me if I would be interested in organising the patients to put on a twenty-minute show for an inter-hospital talent competition. I only had a few months to prepare and I knew that a lot of rehearsals and hard work lay ahead. I began by identifying the patients who could sing, recite, dance or play an instrument. When word got out about the competition, everyone wanted to take part.

As the weeks went by, the performers became more confident, but it was important we stayed within the twenty minutes, otherwise we would be penalised. One member of staff was allowed to be on stage, so I accompanied the patients on the piano. To get the troupe used to performing in front of an audience, I even organised a few dress rehearsals in the hospital's Recreation Hall.

The day for the competition finally arrived and we all set off in the hospital bus for Purdysburn Hospital, Belfast, where the competition was to be held. We were excited, wondering what the other hospital teams were like. However, I knew that it was important to try and keep the patients as calm as possible. On arrival at Purdysburn, we were ushered into the canteen for a light lunch and I set off to find out from the organisers what time we were to be on stage. I saw the judges were already in place, sitting at a table half way down the large hall, so I returned to assemble my troupe and get them ready for their performance.

As we gathered backstage preparing to go on, I assured my performers that they were just as good as any of the other hospitals' competitors. At that point, one male patient who played the accordion said, 'I don't want to play in front of them ones looking at me.' So I had to place him partially behind a stage curtain. Our fiddler, who had taken part from the very beginning in all the rehearsals with the group, decided at the last minute that he wasn't going to take part. Nothing would induce him onto that stage. Another female patient, who was to sing "The Spinning Wheel", was very nervous, so I stayed beside her just in case of a breakdown. Finally it was curtain up and we were on and live. We stayed within the stipulated time and at the end of our act, we got a really good round of applause. We then took our place in the seats reserved for us and watched the rest of the competitors. I tried to guess where we might be placed in the competition. Some of the other acts had lots of fancy dress, but not much talent, while others went over the allocated twenty minutes. I had a sense that our performers did better because of their background in rural homes without television, where improvised entertainment in the form of music and song would have been normal. We had the only performers playing music on instruments.

Finally, the principal judge took to the stage to read out the results. He commented on the "very slick show" of the Tyrone and Fermanagh Hospital troupe from Omagh and we were awarded a cup for having the best solo artist. Overall, we came second, beaten only by half a point! We were delighted with the result, of course. On the way home, we stopped for a little celebration at our "local" on the outskirts of Omagh, the Village Inn in Killyclogher, and we certainly felt that we had earned it! On hearing our good news, the Matron was delighted also and she congratulated us. That was that. At this time, giving extra rewards to staff who went beyond the call of duty would not have been very high on Matron's list of priorities. But virtue is its own reward and it was a huge boost to the patients' morale and to the staff also.

Chapter 18

John and Mary

John and I both enjoyed entertaining people and as we carved out our own niche in the showbusiness world, we also made some great friends, including Margo and Daniel O'Donnell from Donegal, as well as Arty McGlynn, Brian Coll from Omagh and also well known radio presenter Pio McCann. With the experience we had already gained playing at The Market Bar, we began to take on more and bigger venues. We also invested in new equipment, giving us a better quality of sound. But even as we developed our act, we could hardly dream we were to become so popular that our diary was soon filled for a full year with advance bookings.

There were interruptions along the way to showbusiness success. For instance, because I was "off the road" for a while during my two periods of pregnancy and maternity leave, John had to find replacement musicians. Some of those who took on my role were Patsy McCann, Martin Cunningham, Aidan O'Kane and Willie Muldoon. However, I knew it was only a matter of time before I could return to the entertainment scene and we would be back to our original duo as "John and Mary". This would mean that I would have a very busy life. I was first and foremost a wife and mother, but I also had a full-time job at the Tyrone and Fermanagh Hospital and I was a professional entertainer too. The truth is, I loved all of it!

Adjustments and arrangements had to be made. I couldn't expect "Gran" to babysit at night as well, so I knew that I would have to look for another childminder who wouldn't mind late hours. It turned out that a neighbour, Susie Connolly, offered her services. She also had several capable daughters to help out at minding our children, so I had plenty of back-up there. I also had the support of my friends and family, as well as from John, and they all encouraged me to return to the entertainment scene.

I usually arrived home from work at about 5.30pm. After leaving Gran home in the Bluebird, I then had the next few hours to spend with my family. This allowed me time to prepare an evening meal and get Aidan and Sean to bed – which sometimes proved difficult. After changing into our stage clothes, John and I then headed off to play somewhere. The actual playing was only part of our evening's work. We first had to travel to the venue, then we had to allow about thirty minutes to get "set up" and make a sound check. I helped John to carry in the equipment, which consisted of amplifiers, speakers, mike stands, organ, guitar, accordion and a bag of electrical leads. We got into a routine where I could connect up the amplification while John carried in the heavier equipment. Very often it had to be carried upstairs at the venue and, after our performance, it all had to come back down again for our return journey home. This was our routine for five to seven nights of the week and we often played at a wedding on the Saturday as well.

On an average week, we travelled up to 150 miles as an entertainment act. However, this varied and during the winter months and especially around Christmas, we tried to play only at the local venues. In the beginning, our audience was always seated in the new lounges that had been added to the traditional pubs all over the country. As the years went by, a small space for dancing was created up at the front near the small stages on which we performed. That was certainly good for the punters who enjoyed their night out dancing. However, the owners were less enthusiastic and one even said to us, 'When they're dancing they're not drinking.'

For our part, we preferred to play for dancing audiences and, once we found out what they wanted, we varied our programme accordingly. In some venues, for instance, they liked the traditional music that John played on his accordion, while others preferred the Country music, especially the duets we sang. We tried to keep up with the most popular songs of the moment and at weddings, we had a range of special songs to suit the occasion.

Sometimes, without knowing, John and I learned off the same songs and we would both want to sing it in our own style. A bit of a fall out would ensue, but only for professional reasons, of course, and in the interests of "domestic harmony", I usually won out in the end and John stepped back into providing harmony. I remember one such tiff over "The Rose of Allendale". Another problem arose with the famous John Denver song "Country Roads", which was the really big song of the 1970s. I was very keen to start singing it as part of our act, but John is a bit of a perfectionist when it comes to music. 'Don't sing it until we have a bit more practice done on it,' he warned me. The following night, we were playing in Omagh at The Coach Inn and as we came to the last few numbers, I broke into "Country Roads" and John had to follow me along then. I got through it and ended to loud applause from our audience, much to John's annoyance.

Other professional difficulties often arose on the lounge bar circuit when one of the audience would be requested to sing by his "fans". The usual problem, however, was that most of these impromptu performers were very hard to get off the stage once they had started. With the aid of a few drinks, shyness was seldom a factor. Meanwhile, at weddings, our usual arrangement was to get paid at the beginning of the act. Once or twice, for various reasons, this didn't happen and while I packed up after the entertainment, John would set off to hunt down the best man who in the merriment of the occasion would have forgotten completely about our fee.

Our showbusiness career coincided with the height of the Troubles in Northern Ireland, so we were stopped regularly by the security forces on both sides of the border. This was the norm at that time when drivers were often simply "pulled in" to check their identity papers and travel plans. Occasionally, we were ordered to unpack the equipment for inspection and then re-pack the car for a second time before going on to our booking. On such occasions, I could hear John muttering a few "prayers" under his breath!

There were other dramatic moments amidst all the turmoil of the Troubles. We were playing in a lounge bar in Newtownbutler, County Fermanagh, on one occasion and after a short time into our programme, there was a power cut. Since we had a large crowd in that night and we were afraid of panic in the darkness, we decided we had to keep the show going by candlelight. So we performed the rest of the night, singing without microphones. John doubled up by alternately playing the accordion and fiddle, while I accompanied him on acoustic guitar. Through sheer effort and improvisation, we got through the entire night and we even got a standing ovation for our showmanship! This happened to be our first night in that particular lounge bar; after our debut performance, we could do no wrong for our faithful audience there on our many return appearances.

Some places were easier to play than others, but after some time on the road, and a bit more experience, John and I only took bookings for the places we liked. We each had a diary to keep track of our bookings, just in case we double-booked. We also managed ourselves and John usually took care of getting the payment, while I was more involved in the bookings. If someone called our advertised number to make a booking and asked to speak to our manager, I would answer, 'You're talking to her!'

The showbands were still in their hey-day when we started off on the entertainment business, of course, and a lot of the big bands began to use "relief" groups to play for about two hours before they came on stage. Their managers would have arranged this. Barney Curley of Irvinestown, County Fermanagh, who has become best known as a professional gambler and horse trainer, approached us. Barney was manager for a number of showbands in the early 1970s, including The Claxtons and the hugely successful Omagh-based Frankie McBride and the Polka Dots who got into the top of the British charts. Barney engaged us to do relief at various venues before his acts came on. So with the addition of Charlie Gormley on drums, Martin Cunningham on lead guitar, John on rhythm and me as the lead singer, we took to the stage as the four-piece relief band for several of the leading showbands of the time.

I particularly remember playing "relief" for Eileen Reid and the Cadets at the Patrician Hall in Carrickmore and also playing relief for Brian Coll and the Buckaroos at the Astoria Ballroom in Bundoran. No matter who the main act was on such nights, it was a great experience just to sing and play using their fantastic equipment. We got a great buzz performing on these stages and meeting the professional entertainers.

When we played "relief" for one of his showbands, Barney always collected us at our "Chapel House" in Dromore and then drove us to the venue in his big Peugeot car. These dates were usually for Saturday nights, which meant we were very late getting home. But we had Sunday to recover before returning to our full-time work on Monday. On one particular occasion, Barney wanted us to play on a Sunday night and we told him that we would only perform if it was a local venue. He assured us it was, 'Only across the border.' He picked us up in Dromore County Tyrone and we set off in his car. The time passed and finally I looked out the window and saw a stretch of water. I then asked Barney where we were. 'Blackrock, County Louth,' he replied and I realised that we were almost a hundred miles from home. So much for the venue being just "across the border"; Barney hadn't revealed which part of the border he meant! That night we played relief to Frankie McBride and the Polka Dots, but after a few more dates, we decided to discontinue playing "relief". It simply involved too much travelling, too many late nights and, most importantly, being too far from home and our babies.

Yet the lure of showbusiness continued, as we were still involved in the local entertainment scene. A professional manager approached us one night and said he would be interested in forming a band with John and I as the lead singers. We said no to this because we still wanted to hold onto our day jobs. Looking back now, I sometimes wonder if we had taken up his offer, would we have been a success on the showband scene. Except for such occasional dreams, we were happy enough to remain on the lounge bar circuit as "John and Mary".

Chapter 19

Changing with the times

Back in Fivemiletown, my family was changing as the years slipped by and each of my younger siblings slowly began to lead their own separate lives as adults. My younger brother Brian had taken over the running of the farm and my parents were now taking life a bit easier. Una chose the religious life and entered a convent in Mullingar, while Madeline was at a teaching college in London. John was long settled in London by then and the youngest, Kevin, meanwhile, was a day pupil at St Michael's College, the Catholic grammar school for boys in Enniskillen. In time, he joined the civil service and also got married.

Yet while our lives were beginning to unfold as they should, there was dramatic change too. Daddy died very suddenly in 1973, still in his fifties, and his passing left a huge hole in our family where he had always been such a pivotal figure and source of joy with his singing. The entire community in Fivemiletown and far beyond the Clogher Valley, mourned his premature passing at a huge funeral. Daddy had been a great supporter of the local farming community and he was well-known for his knowledge about animals, especially cattle. I can recall people knocking on our bedroom windows at all hours of the night calling, 'Barney can you come as quick as you can? I have a cow calving and she's in trouble.'

Daddy would always recognise the neighbour's voice and call out in reply, 'I'll be there as quick as I can.' This saved our neighbours calling out the vet who would have been expensive to pay. Daddy's services, of course, came free for these emergencies. All of those he helped down the years and those to whom he had brought great joy with his singing and his warm personality came to his funeral.

I recall being almost numbed by the loss of my daddy, but there was more in store. My beloved father-in-law Frank died in the spring of 1974. He had been such a wonderful support to John and me and his love of music and his company had brightened even our darkest days in the beginning of our life together. Frank's death meant the loss of the "Chapel House" in Dromore which had to be vacated for his successor as Sexton. So we bought a bungalow in Omagh where we still live today. That move meant we had to say our sad goodbye to Gran and a lot of good friends, but we promised to keep in touch. At the same time, it was great to be now living nearer to the hospital and not have to travel the ten-mile journey to and from work every day, as I had done for the past eight years. I particularly appreciated this on cold winter months. It also meant that I could come home during my lunch break to catch up on some housework. John, meanwhile, also shortened his commute to work when he secured a job at the Nestlé factory on Omagh's Derry Road. Susie Connolly remained as our babysitter for nights and she came by bus from Dromore to Omagh when needed. When we returned home from playing somewhere, John would then leave Susie home to Dromore.

Aidan was now six and Sean was five years old and both were enrolled in the local St Colmcille's Primary School in Brook Street, Omagh. In the evening, John and I had more time to spend with the boys and help them with homework. My little car, "Bluebird", was a very popular mode of transport to school for our two boys and also for a few of their neighbouring school pals. They all piled in beside me and when we reached the school and the car door opened to let them out, I sometimes saw the look of amazement on the face of the "lollipop lady" school traffic warden! I had a good laugh at that as I drove off. On their return from school in the afternoons, a neighbour looked after the boys until John and I returned from our respective jobs. This meant that during school terms at least, we only needed a childminder for the nights when we were out entertaining.

We had such a busy lifestyle, yet both John and I tried to spend as much time as possible with our two boys. We bought a family caravan, which we kept near the magnificent beach in Rossnowlagh, County Donegal, and that gave us plenty of opportunity to spend holidays as a family and take advantage of any good weather that came along. So during the school holidays every summer, we took a break from the entertainment business and spent a few weeks in Rossnowlagh. While the boys and John played on the beach, I took off my limbs and paddled about on my knees in the waves. I found the salt water was a great relief for irritation or pain in my stumps. I longed to be able to swim, but I doubted that this could ever be possible for a double amputee.

Then in the evenings, we travelled as a family into Bundoran and listened to different groups performing in the local venues there, such as the O'Gorman Arms and the Palace, both of which are now gone. Sean was always more interested in the drummer than in the other members of the group, while Aidan was more taken by the guitar playing. For John and me, it was a pleasant change to sit and listen to someone else performing although, occasionally, we were recognised by someone in the audience and called upon to entertain.

No holiday in Donegal would be complete for us without a visit to the Amusements in Bundoran and top of the list there were the "bumping cars". We paired off – John with Sean and me with Aidan – and had great fun bumping into each other's cars. Aidan certainly fancied himself as a driver on these occasions. Then to finish off the summer holidays, the boys would have one last donkey ride along the beach.

Sometimes when we were playing at a wedding in the South Donegal area, we brought the boys with us and then had an overnight stop in the caravan. As parents, we cherished all of this time we spent with the boys, because we felt even then that they were growing up so quickly. However, during the summer months, Aidan and Sean always looked forward to a few weeks on the farm in Fivemiletown. We tried to make this visit coincide with our busiest weeks of entertainment bookings, especially for weddings when we played as many as three in one week during the high season.

As our showbusiness career grew and prospered, we invested in an electronic keyboard and an automatic drum machine to enhance our sound on stage. The keyboard also meant that I could sit on a high stool while playing. Until then, I had to stand for the full two hours on stage, so it was a great relief to be able to take the weight off my knees and limbs. With the electronic drum machine, we now had a much fuller sound as a three-piece act. The first night we used it, the audience could hear the beat but couldn't see any drums or drummer. They were a bit puzzled at first, but John was an experienced drummer and he had no difficulty setting the machine for the different beats. Over the following years, other acts caught on and invested in a drum machine themselves.

We were constantly changing our programme also, adding songs to our repertoire, honing our performance style. We practised as often as we could, sorting out the keys and chords of our new songs and making sure our delivery was as perfect as we could manage to make it. We liked to specialise in American Country music. Some of our popular duets were "Mrs and Mrs Used to Be" (a George Jones and Melba Montgomery duet), "Crying Time Again", "Silver Sandals,

Greener Pastures", and John also sang the songs of Jim Reeves, Don Williams, Hank Williams, Moe Bandy and Johnny Cash. I liked to perform the songs of Patsy Cline, Jean Shepard, Loretta Lynn, Philomena Begley and Margo (O'Donnell), often learning up to five new songs a week. In all duets, John sang the harmony and very often, we were still practising in the car as we travelled to the venue.

As a result of constant revision, we now had a very varied programme to suit different types of performance. This included John playing traditional Irish music selections on the accordion, while also including American Country barn dance tunes and Scottish Highlands. Meanwhile, my voice was very similar to showband star Margo's, so I concentrated on singing her ballads, which proved to be very popular with our audiences. Margo, her brother Daniel O'Donnell and their mother called to see us in Omagh. I remember giving Margo the words of the celebrated local song by Felix Kearney, "The Hills Above Drumquin" because she was planning to sing it on her next album. In return, she sent me the words of "My Own Dear Galway Bay". At the time, John and I were the only husband and wife duo on the local entertainment scene and most other groups consisted of three or four members. We were confident however that we could more than hold our own with an act that was every bit as strong as our marriage.

Chapter 20

Coping with the Troubles

As we gathered more and more experience in showbusiness, we worked constantly to make our act as good as possible. However, we faced other challenges over which we had little or no control. The Troubles were still raging in Northern Ireland, of course, and this created circumstances that entertainers like us did not have to deal with elsewhere. For instance, many of the towns in which we played had security barriers preventing access to the town centre as a deterrent to car bombings. Because many of the lounge bar venues were inside the barriers, we had to arrange to get through with our equipment by phoning the police and arranging a specific time to get in and another specific time to get out.

Often we had to wait quite a while before the police officers came along to open these gates and let us through when we were going to those venues and then even longer when we were leaving for home. It was quite an ordeal to just sit there waiting, especially in the winter time. It was a problem we didn't have when we played across the border so we did our best to ensure that our bookings were as close as possible to Omagh, especially during the winter months. That also reduced the obvious risk of travelling long distances at night when there was a constant risk of being stopped or diverted by security checkpoints, bomb scares or even worse.

Wedding bookings really suited us because most of these were on Saturdays and many of those we were engaged to play at were in the three Omagh hotels, The Royal Arms, The Silverbirch and Knock-na-Moe Castle, which was the scene of a huge and deadly bombing in 1973 when five British soldiers were killed there. Along with the Royal Arms, the Knock-na-Moe no longer exists. Music for the wedding receptions at that time usually commenced at around 3pm and was finished by 6.30pm at the latest when the bride and groom left on honeymoon and the guests went home. Our two sons and their three pals, Lawrence, William and Noel Lowe, were always delighted with these home venues because they would be asked to help carry in the amplifiers and other equipment. This gave them a good chance to see inside the various venues and earn some pocket money at the same time. They must have been the youngest roadies on the road at that time. Then when all the equipment was on stage, John would begin to wire up and get tuned. Meanwhile, I would drive our young roadies the short distance back to the Lowes' house in my "Bluebird", where Aidan and Sean were looked after I drove back to the hotel, played with John for the next few hours and then we all headed home. If we had two engagements on the same day, which sometimes occurred on Saturdays, we tried to arrange it so that the two venues were as close as possible to avoid long hours on the road. I remember one Saturday, I sang some hymns in Langfield Church at Drumquin, County Tyrone, then travelled with John to play at a wedding reception across the border in the Sandhouse Hotel, Rossnowlagh, County Donegal, and then finally back to Drumquin where we played in O'Kanes' Lounge that night. Three dates on one day, it was tough and demanding showbusiness!

About this time, John and I auditioned for a BBC Radio Show called "Travelling Folk". The auditions took place in the Knock-na-Moe Castle and a lot of other local singers and entertainers also took part. When it came to our turn, Martin Cunningham played lead guitar, John played rhythm and we sang "Everybody's Somebody's Fool". We were successful and then we had to return in a few days to make the recording for the BBC. The day our broadcast was aired on the radio, I was at work and it felt great to hear our performance "on the air". The patients were thrilled and many of them said that I should make a record.

Another night, while John and I were entertaining in a lounge bar in the village of Pettigo, County Donegal, a TV crew approached us and asked if we would take part in a documentary they were making. It was about how the conflict in Northern Ireland at that time was affecting businesses in the border areas. The TV people told us to just play as normal while they filmed. I remember that I was quite nervous about this, but John was not unduly bothered, as he had appeared on TV before with the Noel Hackett Ceilidh Band when it won the Ulster Fleadh Cheoil championship. A few months later, when the documentary was screened, it was such a thrill to see ourselves performing on the TV.

As in every aspect of life, there were occasional mishaps. These ranged from the relatively minor to the near disastrous. Among the former, I recall one particular night when we were setting up on stage, we discovered that one key on the keyboard was jammed and it would totally ruin our performance. I continued to set up the equipment and do the sound checks, while John worked frantically to repair the keyboard, which he managed to do just in time. Among the more serious accidents, the worst happened on a night when we were returning from playing at a New Year's Eve celebration in Toals' of Pomeroy. Just as we reached the fringe of Carrickmore, we hit a patch of black ice on the road. Both the car and the trailer we towed with our equipment went into a tailspin, careered off the road and landed upside down after diving about fifteen feet into a field below the road.

We were so lucky that neither of us sustained any major injuries and we clambered from the car with only a few cuts and bruises.

However, we were both badly shaken and in a state of shock. After climbing out of the car, we slowly made our way back up onto the road and flagged down a passing car. The driver gave us a lift back to Toals' lounge bar where we had played and where the staff were still clearing up after the night. We weren't too happy about leaving the trailer and John was keen to find out how much damage had been done to our expensive equipment. The bar owner then kindly offered to help John transfer all the equipment from the trailer into his estate car and he gave us a lift home to Omagh. There were no mobile phones in those days of course and it was always difficult to find a way to contact home and explain what had happened to keep us so late. Apart from being lucky not to sustain major injuries or even be killed in that accident, we were also relieved to find that we only had to replace a few items from our equipment trailer.

Next morning, John went in search of someone to haul both and car and trailer out of the field. Eventually he got in touch with a local man who had a digger and the car and trailer were taken to a garage. While the car was being fixed, we had to hire out a replacement so we could keep our bookings. To our delight, the equipment was fine and our trailer was back on the road the following week. However, word soon spread that "John and Mary" had been in a serious accident and the phone was hopping for the next few days as well-wishers rang to check on us.

I suppose that news of our accident was a break from the Troubles that enveloped our lives and those of our neighbours. Yet we built up such a resilience in those days that we came to regard the violent unrest, the uncertainty and the pervading threat as normal. I remember that Gallens' Lounge in Castlederg was one of our favourite places to play. It was right on The Diamond in a border community that would take on the unenviable title of the "most bombed town in Northern Ireland". One night we were playing there and everything was going well with our audience enjoying themselves. Then the owner Mickey Gallen came through the door from the front bar waving his hands in the air. He sped across the dance floor shouting, 'Everyone out, it's a bomb.' We all scurried out the back door and huddled together in the backyard waiting for the blast, unable or too scared to move elsewhere because we might be walking into even more risk. I recall it was a cold winter night as we waited for the explosion until eventually, a police and army inspection found the device was a "hoax bomb". We were all glad to get back inside out of the cold, but the night was ruined. Most of the patrons had enough and decided to go home. We did the same.

I suppose like everybody else we knew in the entertainment business in Tyrone and elsewhere across Northern Ireland, there was always a huge bonus in getting a booking for an engagement across the border in those days. Somehow we sensed the change in atmosphere as soon as we drove into Lifford, Pettigo, or even through the checkpoints at Belleek and Aughnacloy. Although we had learned to cope with the pervading uncertainty of the Troubles in the North, we relaxed as soon as we got across the border. There were times when the engagement was even more special.

When my old school friend and neighbour Dympna Keenan asked me to sing at the Mass for her wedding in Monaghan, it was my first time singing in a cathedral. The prospect was quite daunting enough and then I learned that Bishop Patrick Mulligan of Clogher was saying the Nuptial Mass himself. Dympna had been the bishop's housekeeper in Monaghan for several years. On the day of the wedding, I didn't have time to practice with the organist, but everything went off without a hitch and I performed the popular hymns for that time which were "Amazing Grace", "How Great Thou

Art", "The Joys of Love", and "The Wedding Song". After the Mass we just went around the corner from the Cathedral to the Hillgrove Hotel, where John and I played for the wedding reception.

By then we were bringing our two sons with us to the engagements whenever possible. We realised that both the boys showed musical talents from an early age and there was every likelihood that they would follow in our footsteps. Aidan was most drawn to the bass guitar, while Sean had a huge interest in both the drums and guitar. So as they got older, we began to include them in our act and they played with us at concerts, private parties and weddings. Eventually both boys went on to play in bands and groups in their adult life.

Meanwhile, John's job at the Nestlé plant entailed a lot of shift work and this meant we had to curtail our engagements. Most of our bookings were by then for Saturday nights. The schedule eased off and we were content to let it go. Age was beginning to catch up with us and we found that engagements that involved travelling, setting up, then two hours or more on the stage, before packing up and going home, were beginning to take their toll. We had entertained audiences through the best years of the singing lounges, and discos and karaoke machines were replacing live music. This didn't appeal to everyone, of course, especially to the older generation. From time to time, we meet people who remind us of the "great music" we played at their weddings many years ago.

Chapter 21

Getting about

Stanley Millar, a good friend and colleague from the Salaries and Wages office at the Tyrone and Fermanagh Hospital, was confined to a wheelchair after sustaining a serious injury while playing rugby as a young man. However, you would never know that when he was driving about town. He had a car that had been specially adapted and fitted with hand controls. Stanley encouraged me to get one too, but it was a daunting task. First, there were few automatic cars about at the time, compared to the numbers on the road today. So John and I purchased a car with a manual transmission. It was a four door Nissan saloon and we bought it from Grugan's Garage in Omagh, where there were a lot of other second-hand cars to choose from in the showroom. John advised me to sit into the driver's seat and find out what it felt like compared to my little three-wheeler "Bluebird". He knew it was important for me to have room for my limbs and to be in a comfortable position for driving, not cramped. I sat in and it felt great to be behind the wheel of an ordinary car. So after he sorted out the purchase price, John took over the steering wheel and drove us home.

The next thing was to buy the hand controls which were only available in England at the time, and they were very expensive. Then we had to find a competent mechanic to fit them, as they were quite complicated. Eventually, Dermot Grugan from the garage where we bought the car, came to my rescue. He said it would take quite a while to fit them because he had never done a job like this before and he couldn't afford to dedicate all his time to the task because he had to ensure his regular customers were serviced. As a result, my car and controls were relegated to a corner of Dermot's workshop where he would do a bit of work on them when he had the time. I wondered if I had made the right decision in deciding to give up "Bluebird", but I was determined to drive this car and pass my driving test.

Four weeks passed and, eventually, the day arrived when the car was ready to leave the garage. John drove the car home, while I sat beside him wondering how long it would take me to get used to this new car and its strange hand controls. It seemed so big in comparison to the little three-wheeler that I had driven for so long.

It had been quite a while since I had learned to drive "Bluebird" and for that I had to do a full test and learn the Highway Code. At the time, I found the test very easy and I passed with flying colours. However, the licence I was awarded only allowed me to drive in a three-wheeler vehicle. So for my new Nissan, which was also blue although a different shade, I would have to pass a further test before driving it unaccompanied by a fully qualified driver such as John.

For the next few months, I continued driving to work in "Bluebird", while spending my evenings learning to drive the new car with John as my instructor. I became more familiar with the hand controls as those months went by, until I finally found it more comfortable than the three-wheeler. One day when John wasn't about to accompany me in the new car, I decided to drive unaccompanied. It felt great. First I manoeuvred the car out of the driveway and drove down onto a minor road where I could practise and fine-tune my driving. After a period, I felt confident enough to drive through traffic and into the town centre.

Every so often meanwhile, I called round to visit Stanley Miller during my lunch break. He always asked how my driving was progressing. Eventually, I decided to take driving lessons from John McGlade, a registered driving instructor to prepare me finally for my test. I soon realised how much of the Highway Code I had to learn and I knew I would have to improve my driving skills to pass the test. After some lessons with John McGlade, I applied for the test and a date was set. Never averse to challenging myself, I became determined to pass it on the first attempt, although John kept assuring me, 'You can always do it again.' Thankfully, my hard work and determination paid off and I passed first time.

Shortly afterwards, I notified the relevant government authorities in the Department of Health and Social Services that I no longer needed my little three-wheeler. My two sons and their pals were reluctant to see "Bluebird" go as we had spent many happy hours driving about in it. Far from being embarrassed by how different it looked from other cars, I found my children and indeed all other children I came across were delighted by the novelty of "Bluebird". I too was sad to see it go, while at the same time, I was excited to drive around in my new Nissan. It was just the first of many cars to be fitted with hand controls that I have driven since.

In the late 1980s, I joined the wonderful "Motability Scheme" under which I get a new automatic car every three years, fully taxed and insured with ongoing free road services. It is such a change from back then because every time I changed a car, the old controls had to be removed and fitted in the new vehicle.

The problem today is that there is such a selection of cars to choose from and it is often difficult to make up my mind. Some of the cars require no deposit, although the more expensive models do need an up-front payment. The three-yearly choice of replacement has provided lots of family entertainment down the years, especially for my sons who loved to browse over the Motability List that I had to choose from. 'Mammy,' they would plead, 'get a real big fancy car this time, like a Mercedes.' I have resisted their pleas, and down the years I have driven Ford, Vauxhall, Volkswagen, Nissan, Honda and Peugeot. I loved them all for different reasons. Yet sometimes, especially when I forget those cold winter drives from Dromore in my early days, I still long to be setting off down the road on three wheels behind those funny handlebar controls, with my boys and their childhood pals packed into an excited huddle in the back of my Bluebird.

Chapter 22

Open doors

Changes in the guidelines and policies for psychiatric care during the 1970s led to more patients being allowed "parole". At the Tyrone and Fermanagh Hospital this meant increased freedom to move around the grounds, regular home visits for patients and participation in other areas of work both in the hospital and outside. The farm works ceased and the herd of cows was sold off. Many of the male patients were sad to see this happen, especially those from a farming background who had been most involved in the farm itself. At the same time, however, the Industrial Therapy Department was set up at the Tyrone and Fermanagh and Dermot Leonard managed this. The new department was located away from the hospital itself at Lisnamallard on Woodside Avenue, where the old Omagh General Hospital had been when my two boys were born. At Lisnamallard, work was carried out for local businesses. For example, they made garden furniture and did picture framing which was very popular with local artists. Meanwhile, a new printing works was set up in the Tyrone and Fermanagh Hospital grounds managed by Billy O'Donnell. Here patients helped to print material for the hospital's Records Department, the laundry, as well as hospital menus. They also did work for some local businesses as well.

The changes also meant more emphasis on treating patients in the community. This led to a multi-disciplinary approach involving occupational therapists, psychologists, doctors, senior nurses and social workers who assessed each patient's suitability to live out in the community. Newly qualified occupational therapists Irene Boyd and Eleanor Smyth joined the department and became involved in this rehabilitation programme. To prepare patients for living in outside sheltered accommodation, a halfway house was set up within the grounds of the hospital. Patients living there carried on their daily lives with minimal supervision. This prepared them for independent living back in the community where more nurses were now assigned to working with patients in their own homes. Some patients, of course, had no homes or families to return to having been hospitalised for many years. So four houses in Omagh's Strathroy estate were secured from the Northern Ireland Housing Executive. Supervised by a home warden, the former patients got their own private accommodation in Strathroy and were able to live a more normal life. In the first two years of this policy implementation, the Tyrone and Fermanagh's register of patients dropped by a third, from 1,200 to 800 and the reduction continued thereafter.

Through all these changes, I remained in the Arts and Crafts department where more staff members were assigned to work. But things were stirred up there too when the Matron told us we were entering a craft competition between Northern Ireland's eight psychiatric hospitals. Both patients and staff were excited and soon we were in the thick of plans to produce our best craftwork in the categories we chose from the list of suggestions. As some patients had been transferred to the rehab programme, staff members were able to give more individual attention to the remaining patients. It was important to include all patients, of course, including those with lesser skills. On her daily visits, the Matron was keen to see how we were coming along with our entry.

Over the years, I had got to know patients who had reached a high standard in the different crafts. Lawrence, in particular, excelled in basketry and was managing intricate weaves to produce some lovely cane work. This was also my favourite craft, so we worked together in designing something special for the competition. Lawrence was so interested in his work that he often took it back to the ward at weekends to pass the time. Meanwhile, many of the women from rural backgrounds were already competent knitters. Josie was particularly keen on knitting and could follow a difficult pattern for an Aran sweater, for instance. Sometimes, however, she would make a mistake and lose her place in the pattern. I would then have to get her back on track. Josie was very impatient, so while I was working it out, she would hover over me until I got it fixed. While I worked, Josie would abruptly tell anyone else wanting my attention to wait.

We also had a short-stay patient at this time who was an accomplished artist. He produced some wonderful paintings for the competition. With this line-up, we had a core of great work, but I knew that original ideas would get extra points. So we covered old wine bottles with seashells that had been collected by the patients while on holidays at Fleming House in Bundoran, and we made the bottles into table lamps with shades to match. Also in one of the categories we chose, instead of using standard toy kits, Staff Nurse Sally McGrenaghan made our own patterns for the patients to sew. These produced some lovely toys and yet another original idea for our entry. For rug-making, meanwhile, we used uncut Axminister wool. This gave a patient the job of cutting the wool, a simple task but in the patients' eyes, it was a very important job and it made sure that everybody was included in our bid for success.

The day of the competition arrived eventually. We packed all our craft work into the hospital bus and patients and staff set off for Hollywood Hospital in County Down. On arrival we began to carry in our entries and, at the same time, we eyed up the opposition. There was a great air of excitement in the large hall as patients and staff from the competing hospitals mingled and exchanged ideas. The standard of entries was very high and the organisers checked to see that all were in their proper sections. Then we all had to leave the hall while the judging took place.

When we were allowed to return, I found that we had won the competition. In fact, we had accumulated the greatest amount of points (98) with eight firsts, ten seconds and overall first place for the cup. We even won a second cup for the "New Ideas" category. But the looks of delight on the patients' faces was reward enough for all our hard work. After the formal presentation of the cups, there was a short celebration concert with patients and staff called on to entertain. My name was called out to sing a few songs and, on this special day, I was delighted to oblige.

Over the years of working at the Tyrone and Fermanagh Hospital, I had good days and bad days. That day, however, was one of my most memorable. As I removed my artificial limbs with relief that night, I realised I had pressure sores on one of my stumps. In the excitement of the day, I had overdone things a bit. However, once I applied some band-aids to ease the sores and had a good night's rest, I was up and about the following morning, and off to work as usual.

The Matron called into the department to congratulate us on winning our two cups, which were then put on display for everyone in the hospital to see. The local newspapers were contacted and photos and stories about our success featured prominently in them all.

Once the euphoria of winning that important competition had worn off, of course, we realised we had to carry on with the day-today work of the department. But for the next few weeks, we were not under as much pressure as we had been while preparing for the contest, so both patients and staff took it a bit easier. The patients were so delighted at the outcome that they were keen to know when the next competition was taking place. At this stage, we were not even aware that this was to be an annual event. In fact, the following year we went on to win the competition again. This time we didn't have to travel, as the previous year's winner had to host the competition in their own hospital, so as reigning champions in the world of crafts, we had the honour of doing so for the following two years.

Chapter 23

Winding down

When I began to notice that my stumps felt tired, especially after a week's work, I started to wonder how long I could continue in my job. I got my answer sooner than expected. I had a very bad fall at home one evening. It resulted in a dislocated left kneecap and I experienced the most excruciating pain. For the first time in my life, I was confined to a wheelchair because I was unable to wear my artificial limbs and had to undergo several weekly sessions of physiotherapy. By coincidence, the Occupational Therapist who brought me the wheelchair was Ann Slane, with whom I had worked several years earlier and we had a good chat about our years together in the Tyrone and Fermanagh Hospital.

Our two boys Aidan and Sean, were teenagers now and I was glad of their help about the house. A sort of rota was established and when John came home from work, he took over. It was the first time that I had to sit for so long in the same place and I was very impatient. I tried to put on the artificial limbs every morning, but to no avail. My knee was still too painful and it was unable to stand any pressure. To pass the time while sitting in the wheelchair, I started work on a tapestry, not realising that I would have plenty of time to finish it because it was almost four months before I was able to wear my artificial limbs again.

It felt great to be mobile once more, but for the first few days it felt like I was learning to walk all over again. Then when I visited the limb-fitting centre in Belfast, my doctor confirmed that, due to the complete dislocation of my left kneecap, my left stump was now out of line. I had to be measured up for new limbs, with special emphasis being placed on support for the left knee. Although the new limbs seemed comfortable enough, I was still very apprehensive about falling again. That bad fall had certainly shaken my confidence, just as it had slowed me down and left me unable to walk long distances again. So with both my limbs and my body beginning to slow down, I knew that it was inevitable that I would have to retire from my job at the Tyrone and Fermanagh Hospital where I was now in my thirtieth year. Although I was off on sick leave, I called out on a regular basis to see both patients and staff. I then had to explain to the patients that I was no longer able to work and they all expressed disappointment at seeing me leaving. Over many years working in the Occupation Therapy department, I got to know patients who were admitted on a regular basis. Even so, I hadn't realised until I was told, that, on being admitted and examined by the doctor, many of them requested to be sent to "Mary O'Brien's therapy". This bears out the lesson I learned from experience: the more patients are kept occupied, the more content they are.

The staff and patients organised a retirement party and presented me with a gift of a chiming wall clock. I promised the patients that I would call back to see them as often as I could and we all spent a few very pleasant hours reminiscing about my years in the hospital. As I looked around the department for the last time, I was overcome with nostalgia, thinking of the wonderful staff I had worked with and all the patients I had helped. As I drove out of the hospital gates, memories came flooding back, some happy and some sad, but, overall, I realised they were very rewarding years.

With that part of my life over, I now had more time to devote to my husband and family. Our two teenage sons and their friends had formed their own musical group, so I spent some of my time driving them to a local unused barn where they rehearsed, mostly at the weekends. I enjoyed listening as they practiced their music, and I gave them all the encouragement I could. They had such fun as they played and sang the current hits of the day.

Both our sons eventually went on to become very successful musicians in different groups. Sean began drumming when he was about twelve or thirteen, starting with the knife and fork on the table until we bought him his first drum-kit. He drummed as he listened to Gene Krupa, the great American jazz percussionist, but he also went on to drum with his father in St Lawrence's Pipe Band in Fintona. He also learned the clarinet from local musician Tony Mathers. Aidan had already begun playing the bass guitar when he was very young. We bought him his first bass, a Fender Precision, from Pio McGartland, a member of the then successful Omagh group, Casper. From time to time the boys played with us if we had a big booking, but John and I were too used to playing as a two-piece act and we found it hard to adapt as a four piece.

Soon our home became a very noisy house, with our young neighbour Larry Lowe on lead guitar, another neighbour Cathal McAshee as lead singer, while Chris McGuigan also played the drums. Sean continued his musical career and later went on tour throughout Europe and the USA with the Tyrone band, More Power to Your Elbow. He now plays regularly with other musicians at a Jazz session in Omagh on Monday nights. Aidan, meanwhile, has played with Stockton's Wing.

Chapter 24
PHAB times to take the plunge

In the final years of my working life, I had seen an advertisement in the local papers looking for volunteers to form the local branch of a group called "PHAB", which stands for "Physically Handicapped and Able Bodied". The aim is to integrate people with disabilities into general society through youth clubs and social activities and thereby break down barriers of prejudice. I went along to the first meeting in 1986. It was held in Omagh Youth Centre where an article from the PHAB magazine was read out:

> It is pointless teaching young people with a disability to walk or talk if there is no vocational or social guidance. While it is fantastic to see any young person overcome a disability they will remain stunted psychologically, unless parents allow them to mix socially, gain independence and make their own space.

I strongly believed in those aims and what PHAB was trying to achieve. So I became one of its founder members in Omagh. When our committee was formed of both able-bodied and disabled members, I was chosen as Chairperson, Róisín McConnell became Treasurer and Bernie McCollum was our Secretary. Other committee members were Mairéad McCann, Rosie Meenan, Amanda Murdoch, Perpetua

McNamee and Julie Blackburn and we all put a few pounds into the "kitty" for a bank account. My life was about to take on a whole new meaning. Never even having chaired a meeting before, I was on another steep learning curve. As word spread about the club, members came from a twenty miles radius, including the villages and towns of Beragh, Sixmilecross, Drumquin, Ballygawley, Dromore, Irvinestown and Fintona. With our Omagh town members, the club soon had between thirty and thirty-five members.

We came together every Tuesday night in Omagh Youth Centre and our programme was drawn up with the intention of having something for everyone. Our organised weekends involved outings for both physically handicapped and able-bodied members to wonderful facilities such as the SHARE centre and Castle Archdale in County Fermanagh and Carlingford in County Louth. During these weekends, long-lasting friendships were formed as we taught and encouraged our young people to become more independent.

Of all the PHAB club's activities, swimming proved to be the most popular. It began when I asked at one of our PHAB groups meetings if anyone would be interested in teaching me to swim as I was so keen to learn. Róisín McConnell, then a twenty-year-old student volunteered to take me on. She was a very good swimmer herself, but she had no experience of teaching a disabled person, and especially not a double amputee. But she was up for the challenge with me.

The following Monday after work, Róisín collected me from home and we set out in her car for Strabane Leisure Centre, about twenty miles away. It was her idea to go there for our first lesson because she thought it would be quieter than the pool in Omagh. On the journey, I told Róisín about the accident in which I had lost my legs all those years ago. I believe she got quite a shock at the details and she wondered how I had survived. Yet any misgivings about my resolve to learn to swim were brushed aside when I told her how I had worked all through my life, how I had married and raised two sons and how I was now ready to take on new challenges.

Yet as the Strabane Leisure Centre came into view, I had "butterflies" in my stomach with the nervous excitement and, because I had never been in anything like a leisure centre before, I had to rely on Róisín for guidance, even when I explained to her that I would have to remove my artificial limbs before I got into the pool. We discovered that the changing rooms were quite a distance from the poolside, too far for me to negotiate on my knee stumps. The only alternative was a storeroom, which the attendants said we could use. So I sat on a chair provided by the staff and amidst all the brushes, mops and buckets, I removed my limbs. It never even occurred to me that this was the first time that Róisín had seen an amputee do this, and a double amputee at that. Yet she seemed to take it all in her stride as we got into our swimming costumes. Then we opened the door and I made my way on my knees to the poolside for the very first time in my life. Róisín helped me down into the water and suddenly, my life changed. Never before had I felt such a sense of physical freedom as I did on that first occasion when I got into a pool and began to follow the instructions of my young tutor.

There were moments of confusion, if not hilarity. Róisín kept saying to me, 'Pull with your arms and kick.' I had to keep reminding her that I had nothing to kick with! At first, I found it very difficult to keep my head up from the water, because I had no lower limbs to balance my body. Time and again, my head dropped below the surface and I took in mouthfuls of water as I struggled in shock each time. After several big gulps, however, I learned to pull stronger with my arms to compensate for the lack of rear balance. I was learning by the necessity of not drowning, that amputees are totally reliant on their arms when swimming. Once I became aware of this, I knew what to do, and I did it over and over again.

After about an hour, I knew that I was capable of swimming a good stroke and Róisín began to deflate my armband buoyancy aids. I kept urging her to take them off, and I believe it took her a while to realise how determined I was to get out of them and swim all on my own. Yet I still kept practising and became more confident, until Róisín finally said, 'I don't think you need the armbands anymore.' She pulled them off and at first I missed their support when I discovered I had to work even harder with my arms to stay afloat. I persevered, of course, and soon I was venturing further and further until eventually Róisín and I were swimming side by side and it felt marvellous; so much so that we stayed in the pool for about two hours on that first occasion. I felt both relaxed and exhilarated as I moved through the water. I began with the breaststroke and once I was swimming independently, there was no holding me back. I believe I felt so confident because I never had any fear of water and I was so keen to learn. That first two-hour lesson actually felt more like ten minutes to me because I was enjoying myself so much. We finally emerged from the pool and I felt physically exhausted, but totally elated because of my progress.

Back in Omagh, Róisín and I went swimming together every Tuesday night which was our PHAB club night. Others soon took up the challenge and our club numbers grew, but it meant some lobbying on our part before swimming became accessible for all. Up until then, wheelchair users were unable to avail of the swimming pool facilities at Omagh Leisure Centre. The installation of a hoist solved this problem and once that was in place we organised a "Special Needs Swimming Weekend" with a specialised swimming instructor brought over from England.

It was great also to see most of the club's members taking advantage of this opportunity, especially the disabled members who had most to gain from this great exercise. Swimming is one sport where both able-bodied and disabled people can come together on equal terms. I also found there was great motivation among the leaders and this passed right down to the youngest members in our club.

Afterwards, when word began to spread about our "Disabled Swimming Sessions", I realised that more swimming classes needed to be provided in the greater Omagh area. First I had to find more volunteers so I put another advertisement in the local papers and the first man to answer was Frank Curneen. A retired factory worker who was also qualified in swimming instruction, Frank proved to be an exceptional teacher for disabled swimmers. As our numbers grew, other volunteers who played a pivotal role included Róisín McConnell, Kathleen Cox, Martin Fiddis, Eamon Doherty, Wendy Sterritt, Kathleen Colgan. We soon had a great team and we moved our sessions to Campsie pool in Omagh, a facility owned and operated by the Western Education and Library Board for use by the schools. There we relied on Seamus Haigney, Harry Rodgers and Martin Fiddis to lift the disabled swimmers in and out of the water. These men were professional nurses who had expert knowledge of lifting techniques. The age of participants ranged from ten to seventy. Among them was young Michelle Mullan, the victim of a serious road accident. While still at school Michelle was left paralysed with severe head injuries. When fitted with a special collar and supervised by Kathleen Cox, Michelle spent several hours a week in the pool over the next four years. These weekly sessions really helped her total wellbeing.

Chapter 25

Going for gold

I had always believed that not having lower limbs meant it would be quite a difficult task for me to swim. Up to my involvement with the Omagh PHAB Club, I had never met any disabled swimmers, especially not amputees. In fact I had little real knowledge of this sport because the only time I ever saw competitive swimming was on TV. Once I learned how to swim, I enjoyed it so much that I began to swim for one hour every day, five days a week. In the beginning I was keen to see how fast I could swim, but my coach Frank Curneen said, 'You must first learn the proper technique, then you can swim as fast as you want.'

I soon found out that, for Frank, there was no second best. First I learned the breaststroke and then, several months later, I learned the backstroke. Frank and I persevered until I achieved near perfection in these two swimming strokes. Frank then encouraged me to learn the front crawl (or free-style), which is recognised as the best swimming stroke for amputees. Since I swim totally using my arms, he believed I would excel in it. However, I found the front crawl the most difficult of all strokes to learn because my face was in the water most of the time. Frank encouraged me to stay at it. Eventually, under his guidance – and after spending many long hours in the pool – I became proficient in all three strokes.

Eventually I became capable of swimming one mile (64 lengths of the pool) in an hour. I then became a member of the British Amputee Sports Association (B.A.S.A.). Suddenly I realised that my swimming times were good enough to compete at national level. So I put my name forward to take part in the National Amputee Games, held annually in Stoke Mandeville Centre, Aylesbury, near London. It gave me a goal to aim for and I prepared for the big event by spending hours in the pool, improving my times and perfecting my stroke.

My coach Frank called on his friend, Tom Flanagan, who had a wealth of experience of coaching at competition level. Although my own strokes were near perfection in technique, I had to learn the proper way to start and finish each individual movement. Under Tom's constant supervision, I learned all I needed to know about competing, again spending hours in the pool, but enjoying every minute of it.

Finally the time came to go to the swimming competition, which was held on 24 June 1990. Frank was unable to travel, so Tom Flanagan accompanied me instead. I was also glad to have Ruth Lockhart, a swimming companion and also an amputee, travelling with me. After an overnight stay with my aunt and uncle in London, we travelled by train to Stoke Mandeville the next morning. I spent some time in the swimming pool, putting in last minute practice and trying to remember all that Frank had taught me: 'Pull, breathe, kick! Breathe out under water, breathe in on top of water.' I had never seen so many amputees in the one place at the same time and, of course, we discussed our life histories, explaining how we lost our limbs. Throughout the complex, there was a great buzz of anticipation.

The next morning, I was delighted when Perpetua McNamee from the Omagh PHAB Club arrived to take us to High Wycombe for the competitions. Tom, Ruth and Perpetua talked to me on the way, helping to calm my nerves. However, when I arrived at the poolside, I froze momentarily when I realised that I had to swim in a 50-metre pool. Up to now, I had done all my training in a 25-metre pool. This was a slight setback but Tom reassured me: 'Just remember all you have been taught. Just give it your all.' After those words, I approached the pool with more confidence.

When my name was called out, I entered the pool for my first event – the backcrawl. 'On your marks, get set, go!' I swam up the pool, my heart pounding, hoping I would make the distance. I did, and hauled myself from the pool. My next event was the breaststroke and, this time, I felt more confident that I would make it to the end. Then after another short interval, we came to my final event – the front crawl, which by now was my favourite stroke and I found myself swimming with even more confidence in that event. On emerging from the pool this time, I was both physically and mentally exhausted. But even so, I realised that all my previous months of training had paid off. I had competed and completed the events. Shortly thereafter, I learned that they had paid off in spades for, not only had I won three gold medals for the three events, I had set three new British national records! My times in the three events were; female backstroke 50 metres, 01:5.49 minutes, 50 metres breaststroke, 01:11.74 minutes, and the freestyle 50 metres, 1:03.76 minutes.

'Well done, well done!' Tom called to me, along with congratulations from Perpetua and Ruth. I basked in my victories, of course, but I couldn't wait to phone everyone at home with my good news – my husband John, my coach Frank and especially my mother. As we emerged from the Leisure Complex, my mind went back to a day on the beach in Bundoran so many years ago when, as a small child, my father lifted me into the little pool. He would have been so proud of me that day.

After my success, I was named Omagh District Council's "Sports Personality of the Year" and Frank Curneen won the "Services to

Sport Award". A video recording of the swimming sessions in Campsie Swimming Pool was produced and it took first place in the "Best Promotional Video (PHAB Club)" from the Western Education and Library Board. Then Carty McGirr from Trillick, who had lost his legs and subsequently danced with me all those years before, now joined me in taking part in the annual British Telecom Swimathon. We swam one hundred lengths each (2,000 metres and we were the only amputees in Northern Ireland to take part in the event.

After my success, my name became synonymous locally with disabled swimmers. With the knowledge I had gained from Frank and Tom, I now began to coach both able-bodied and disabled swimmers on a one-to-one basis every week. My pupils included Heather Cowan from Sixmilecross, Ruth Clarke from Ballygawley, Philip McCandless and Rosie Meenan, both Omagh, Kate McLaughlin, Dromore, and Bernadette McFarland, Fintona.

As well as being chairperson of the Omagh PHAB Club, I was also on its management committee where my organising skills were now being put to the test. First of all, club members, totalling forty by now, were keen to have some social activities such as holidays and day trips.

'We'll first have to do some fundraising,' our treasurer Róisín McConnell informed us. Suggestions poured in; flag days were organised, along with fundraising nights. Local entertainer Dominic Kirwan performed for us, free of charge. A fashion show was organised by Róisín herself and it was held in the Silver Birch Hotel, with most of the PHAB members taking part. I had to compère for the entire show because the scheduled M.C. took ill. It was my first time to do anything like this, but once I had the microphone in my hand I felt fine!

From experience, we found out that the best way of raising funds was a sponsored walk with both the club members and their friends and supporters taking part. I asked a local farmer for a pony and trap for the day. He was delighted to come along and help out 'such a worthy cause.' The first walk began at the car park of the Coach Inn on Omagh's Dromore Road and it ended at Price's Shop in Clanabogan, a distance of about five miles. The pony and trap proved a great success, with everyone wanting a ride in it.

Joe Teague, Dromore, was talked into doing a skydiving fundraiser with a tandem parachute jump. Paralysed from the waist down in a road accident, Joe was the first paraplegic from Northern Ireland to do this jump from 8,000 feet over Garvagh in County Derry. It was on the Northern Ireland television news that evening, so as well as raising a lot of money, it got great recognition for our PHAB club. Then two other young club members, Florence Ewing and Colleen Conway, both profoundly deaf, also completed a fundraising jump with The Wild Geese Parachute Club. We found in all our fund-raising events, the Omagh people were great supporters.

Chapter 26

Spreading our wings

Holidays became the annual highlights of the Omagh PHAB Club's activities. They let our young members experience different cultures, while gaining their own personal independence. In our early days, three of our young members – Anne Marie McKenna, Amanda Murdoch, and Rosemary Meenan – got the holiday of a lifetime in Canada, organised through Northern Ireland PHAB in Belfast. Based at the Variety Village in Scarborough, Ontario, the girls had trips to Niagara Falls, Toronto City Hall, Canada's Wonderland and Ontario Place.

The first of many holidays I organised was to Butlins Holiday Camp at Pwllheli, North Wales. About thirty members went along, ranging in age from sixteen to fifty which included both able-bodied and disabled. It was raining very heavily on the morning we departed. At Dun Laoghaire, the storm was raging and it was very difficult for the wheelchair users to board the ferry without getting soaked, but we managed. The crossing to Holyhead was the roughest in twenty-five years: Instead of two hours, it took four. Most of our group got seasick, including me! 'A good way to begin a holiday,' someone laughed beside me as I heaved my lunch over the side. Then because of our late arrival at Butlins, we also missed our first evening tea. Eventually we got everybody settled down for a good night's sleep.

We awoke to glorious sunshine and, for the rest of the week, we had beautiful weather.

We had plenty of laughs too at Butlins. One of the able-bodied junior members asked, 'Mary can I try on your limbs?' I had to say that they don't work well if you already have limbs. Then another senior member and me were dared to go up on the big dipper. We took up the challenge and we were a bit shaken, but it felt great. For our entire stay, there was great camaraderie between young and old, with everyone trying to play pranks on each other. Then at night we enjoyed the entertainment. Sure enough someone called for 'a song from Mary O'Brien.' I gave them "One Day at a Time" and "Blanket on the Ground". There was a talent competition on the following night. All my friends wanted me to take part, but I declined. By the time we left, however, everyone knew about the Omagh PHAB club from Ireland and we were chosen as the most popular group at the holiday camp.

After that first experience of stepping out into the world, even for those of us with no legs, we were keen to spread our wings even further. Trevor Boyle, Director, Northern Ireland PHAB, came to our monthly meeting in September 1991 and told us about the first conference on disabilities to be held in Eastern Europe. Moscow, he promised, was an opportunity not to be missed! The idea was to bring together disabled people from all over Western Europe and the former Soviet Bloc. This would provide contacts, develop exchanges and projects, share experiences and, above all, emphasise the need for liberty and understanding as the Russian empire collapsed. An air of idealistic excitement filled the room and it wasn't long until twelve Omagh members, including me, signed up to go

Months of planning and preparations lay ahead for the conference which was scheduled to be held from 26 July to 1 August, the following year. We did some fundraising, mainly to help our young travelling members who were still students. We also received a small grant from the Omagh District Council and "Silver Wing Travel" helped, both with our flights to and from Moscow, and with a generous donation towards the trip. Once our passports and visas were checked, we had to plan our transport to and from the Shannon Airport for the Aeroflot flight to Moscow. This was a valuable team-building exercise and the help and cooperation continued throughout the trip.

We finally touched down in Moscow and were met at the airport there by our four Russian guides – Olga, Alla, Svetlana and Dino – who were students at Moscow University. From day one, Olga was the boss. Although she spoke very little "English", we all understood her commands: 'You sit!' 'You go!' 'You wait!' To get us to our hotel, the Orlionok, which was specially built for the Moscow Olympics, a special bus with wheelchair lifts was laid on. We were soon glad that we had only one wheelchair user, because access was very poor outside of the hotel where we were based for the duration of the conference. This meant we had to carry Rosie up and down flights of stairs. Yet every aspect of the conference was thoroughly organised. Around 400 participants represented thirty-two countries. So given all the different languages, communication was difficult. This difficulty was compounded of course, by all those who were deaf or blind, or both. I enjoyed meeting a deaf and blind author, who communicated through two interpreters, one for English and one Russian. I explained that I was from Ireland and he remarked, 'Little green country!'

The conference opened with a Military Brass Band and an open-air display with a selection of Russian stalls and crafts. There was also a display of parachute jumping, sideshows, auctions and a banquet with folk dancing and songs. It was all very colourful. A replica of a Russian Orthodox Church was specially built for the occasion, complete with choir, candles for peace and a traditional Russian service, during which a special message from President Boris Yeltsin was read. I enjoyed the choristers who had very powerful voices. They sang in perfect harmony, mostly unaccompanied. The Russians know how to put on a show and we were all in awe of everything we saw. In the evening, TV crews came to record this special event. Somehow a microphone found its way to me and, with the aid of an interpreter, I appeared on Russian TV that night. I think I said, 'Disabled people are entitled to a life, just like everyone else.' Then to finish off this special day, we were treated to a spectacular fireworks display.

When the conference began, we were able to meet disabled people from many backgrounds and compare our lives with theirs. We learned about attitudes to disability in other countries and this helped us to appreciate what is being done at home for the disabled. We also discovered that "access" was practically unheard of in Russia at that time – no disabled toilets, no ramps for wheelchairs. Social Workers were only being introduced into the Russian system, which was very far behind on safeguarding basic human rights. The vast majority of those with "special needs" from other countries did not get any help, apart from what their families provided. This, of course, compared so unfavourably with our own system of benefits.

I felt so embarrassed when I encountered a young man, a double amputee like myself, whose only means of transport was a skateboard. I thought back over the years to the artificial limbs that I had been provided with, both as a child and adult, supplied by the National Health Service. While embarrassed, I also felt very privileged in comparison to the young amputee.

Our afternoons and evenings in Moscow were spent at stage shows. These included fine musicians and dancers in costume and they were all held in the local exhibition centre. It gave us a glimpse of the rich Russian culture. Among the highlights for me was a display by local gymnasts. Another big event came when our guide Olga, whose efficiency had by now become legendary among delegates, organised a trip to the Moscow State Circus where we watched in awe as the trapeze artists performed and we recoiled in fear from the large Russian bears. Because she was in a wheelchair, Rosie was placed right up beside the circus ring. Whenever the bears began to dance, Rosie looked more than a little uneasy!

Halfway through the week, we went on a boat trip down the Moska River. That whetted our appetite for seeing the city, so we decided to forego the formalities of the conference and spend the last couple of days seeing the sights. This was a one-off trip, so we wanted to cram in as much as we could, especially with the Russian Guides at our disposal. By this stage, of course, we had become widely known as the "Irish Group" with a reputation for enjoying ourselves. Yet our time had been spent mainly at the conference and visiting cultural centres. We wanted more craic, so we all agreed that a bit of "nightlife" was in order. We then used our Irish charm to persuade Olga to take us to the nearest "pub", a place called the Arabat Bar, but known in Russian as "The Irish Bar". With drinks so cheap, the atmosphere soon warmed up and the craic was good. Before long, someone called out, 'Mary, give us a song.' So I started with "The Wild Rover", then sang "The Galway Shawl" and followed this with our local song, "The Hills Above Drumquin". Our Russian guides soon joined in and sang in their native tongue. It was the first time the Russian staff of the Irish bar had experienced a little bit of Irish entertainment! Suddenly we all stopped singing when the owner, a tall Canadian, approached our table. Kate whispered to me, 'This sing-song may not have been a good idea, Mary. We could be arrested!'

The owner smiled broadly however, and called out, 'Keep on with your singing. This is what an Irish pub is all about.' He then signalled for our group to have another round of drinks on the house. As if we hadn't had enough already!

The bar owner later announced that we were to be treated to a free breakfast in McDonald's highly popular Moscow outlet the following morning. I've heard of people singing for their supper; this was the first time I heard of singing for their breakfast. I suppose that is the luck of the Irish!

But our night on the town was not over yet. When we arrived back at the hotel, we continued our celebration. Word soon spread that an "Irish Party" was taking place on the 17th floor. What a night! I learned beyond doubt that music crosses all barriers! People began to arrive from throughout the huge hotel, bringing along their own bottles. With vodka priced at only 40p and champagne at 50p a bottle, it was a night to remember even for those who could not. I do recall that when I was going to bed, I said to my roommate Bernie, 'I'm definitely legless tonight!'

Olga was banging on our bedroom door: 'Come, come, time to go to McDonald's.' As well as a "mild" hangover, I had another reason for lying on in bed. My artificial limbs, which I always keep by my bedside, were missing.

I sent Bernie off around the rooms asking, 'Did anyone see a pair of legs?' I was so glad to eventually strap them on.

By now I was the last of our entire party to get dressed and, in a panic I wrenched open the wardrobe door. Bernie's carrier bag crashed to the floor. Oh, my Lord, what valuables have I broken? On closer examination, it was the bottles of vodka Bernie had planned to bring home. How was I going to explain this catastrophe? But my good friend Bernie simply said, 'They're only 40p a bottle, I'll get some more!'

Eventually, we got to McDonald's where we were ushered by the Canadian owner past the queue for our free breakfast. He told us we could choose whatever we liked from the large menu. So we tucked into burgers, chips and sausages, with ice cream to follow. It was a relief to get our taste buds working again. The food in the hotel was edible but very bland. Breakfast was black tea and very hard bread – no milk or toast. The potatoes were tiny and scarce with small quantities of meat but lots of rice. Our Russian guides really enjoyed the experience of eating at McDonald's; normally it would be too expensive for them to eat there.

With only one day left we decided to visit the Kremlin, a very impressive building. Then we queued for quite a while to see Lenin's Tomb in Red Square where we were not allowed to take photographs. After this, we visited the Palace of Art and Culture, where I saw some great paintings and gold icons, as well as stuffed real horses. Finally, we wanted to see what was left of the Czar's Palace, but there was only a model of it as most of the palace was now in ruins.

Back at the hotel, our four guides invited us to join them in making a toast Russian style. They only drink pure vodka straight, and we were expected to do the same! Unknown to the rest of us, however, my roommate Bernie replaced her vodka with water and set the bottle on the table with the rest. We each drank from our own bottles and I wondered why we were all becoming quite merry while Bernie remained sober. She laughed but said nothing and it was only when we arrived back home that she revealed all!

For our final night, there was a large banquet in the "Russia Hotel". Security was very tight to keep out gatecrashers. All the different nationalities assembled, with each group at their own table in the banquet hall. There was a large variety of food and drinks, with three different types of caviar, which our Russian Guides enjoyed. There were speeches about the success of the festival but, as the wine took effect, the speeches were soon drowned out by groups starting to sing. When "Northern Ireland" was called upon, I had to go up to the stage and make a speech as group leader. I was allowed no wine on this occasion, but all I can remember saying was, 'East finally meets West,' before simply congratulating everyone on a marvellous festival.

As we packed for home later, we became quite emotional in our goodbyes. Olga called me, 'my Irish mother,' and said, 'My lovely Irish group, I miss you.' As a parting gift, I gave Olga a necklace, while our younger members gave t-shirts, modern music tapes and any roubles we had left. We then exchanged addresses and promised to keep in touch. I still have kept all the letters Olga wrote to me.

The sun shone every day while we were in Moscow, but the morning we left, the rain came pouring down. Olga kept saying, 'Russia cries because you go,' all the way to the airport terminal doors where we said our final farewell, because our guides were not allowed to go any further.

One by one, we filed through the airport security system, but when it came to my turn, the machine went 'bleep, bleep...' I was put through a second time and again 'bleep, bleep...' My group was laughing at my predicament, but the Russian security man looked very stern. Our guides were gone; I didn't know any Russian; and he hadn't a word of English. How would I explain about my artificial limbs? Eventually, I lifted up my trouser leg and said, 'Feel, feel – artificial.' It worked, but perhaps it was the KGB hat I was wearing that got me through!

As the plane took off from Moscow, my thoughts wandered back to when I was a small child at Tyreghan school, gazing at the large map of the world on the classroom wall and thinking that the country I most wanted to visit was Russia. My dream had now been fulfilled in the trip of a lifetime. Yet it made us appreciate our own beautiful country and we all agreed that Russia was a great place to visit, but not to live.

Chapter 27

Travels with Mother

I had often heard my mother saying she would love to go to Lourdes sometime. So around the time I retired in 1988, I saw an article in the local Ulster Herald newspaper about a four-day pilgrimage to Lourdes, organised by the Order of Malta's Omagh branch. When I phoned my mother to see if she would like to go, she was thrilled with the prospect. So we set off by coach from Omagh to Dublin airport and flew directly to France, where another coach took us to the centrally located hotel in Lourdes where most of our group was staying. It was May and we were blessed with glorious weather.

My mother and I were both keen to see the Grotto so we set off on that first night with map in hand and negotiated our way through the steep, cobbled streets. At the Grotto, we were both overcome with emotion at the scene as we knelt down to pray, partly because we had never seen so many nationalities all in one place. Displayed on a tree there beside our Lady's statue were crutches, walking sticks and calipers (leg braces), which had been left behind by pilgrims who had been cured there. Observing the custom of lighting candles for our personal intentions and those of our friends and relatives back home, we lit quite a few. Then on our way back to the hotel, we decided to take a shortcut and promptly got lost: so much for my map reading skills! However, that first evening made me realise that I was going to need help getting around for the next few days. The hotel had wheelchairs available for those who needed them, so each morning when the organisers announced the programme for that day, depending on the distance we had to go, I would decide whether I would avail of one of the wheelchairs. I also got a young helper to push me. However, I was advised not to get too near the front of the Grotto; otherwise people might proclaim another "miracle" if I decided to stand up!

We spent our first day in Lourdes going to where Saint Bernadette was born and raised in the old police barracks. We saw where all the same family slept in one room and lived in such poor conditions. Meanwhile, I was looking forward to visiting the Baths. My mother wasn't too keen on the idea, but I coaxed her along and we made our way there. I saw a sign pointing disabled people to a separate entrance, but I decided to stay with my mother and go to the able-bodied baths. When it came to my turn, I went into the changing room and took off both my clothes and my limbs. With only a white sheet covering me, I then lowered myself into the very cold bath. Suddenly there was a great commotion among the attendants when they realised I was an amputee. They pointed out excitedly that I was in the "wrong bath". However, there wasn't much they could do about it now since I was in the water... and enjoying it! Afterwards, I realised that there was no need to bring along a towel because, on emerging from the water, I was dry!

During our pilgrimage to Lourdes, we could spend our nights doing whatever we wanted. I was asked to sing at a party being held in one of the hospitals. It was a considerable distance from our hotel, so I decided to use one of the hotel's wheelchairs. We set off and I was never pushed so quickly in a wheelchair, because my young helper was in a hurry to get to the party. My poor mother had to run alongside! However, we met some very ill patients at the hospital and I felt privileged to be able to help them in any way possible.

I also felt privileged to take part in one of the highlights of our pilgrimage – the candlelight procession to the Grotto. It was a spectacular ceremony to witness with all the pilgrims from different countries praying in their own languages. The procession path was lined with chestnut trees in full blossom and their scent wafted into the night air as we passed along. Also when we visited the large Basilica to attend a special Mass for the sick, we were delighted to hear our own Cardinal Tomas Ó Fiaich celebrating the Eucharist in the Irish language. Two years later, Cardinal Ó Fiaich died in Lourdes while leading another pilgrimage.

Then before returning home, we set off to purchase relics and souvenirs for our friends and relatives back home. We found that Lourdes was very commercialised. The only thing free was Holy Water, which people brought home by the gallons. However, we had to pay for the plastic containers! My mother was delighted with that trip to Lourdes and we met some wonderful people. Some of them told us how many times they visited Lourdes; in some cases, they had been there as many as forty times.

Mother had obviously got the travel bug after that Lourdes trip, so when my younger sister Una was graduating from Boston University Business School in May 1991, she and I went to America for the conferring ceremony. We flew from Dublin with a brief stop at Shannon where we bought a few bottles of duty-free Irish whiskey for Una and her friends. By now, I had learned from experience that going through airports can be a daunting experience for amputees, so I requested help. Once off the plane at Boston, a Logan Airport attendant was there to push me in a wheelchair. Again I was whizzed along and my elderly mother had to trot along on our heels. After collecting our luggage, however, we were both relieved and happy to see Una waiting for us. We stayed with her friends, Peggy Doyle and Una Gillic, in a large two-family house in Roslindale, a leafy residential area of Boston. Everyone wanted to know if we were tired after our flight but I had so much adrenalin pumping through my veins, I was too excited to be tired. It was just as well I had a rush of energy because Una, who does guided tours of Boston, had places of interest for us to visit every day we were there.

We went to the birthplace of John F Kennedy in Brookline where we were given a guided tour of the house, including the very room where the future president was born. The basement kitchen contained two large stone sinks and a massive stove. Our guide explained that this two-storey house would have been looked on as small back in the days when the Kennedys lived there. In comparison to our own houses in Ireland, it seemed like a mansion!

One evening, other friends of Una's invited us to a concert of the famous Boston Pops Orchestra. Our evening began at a very exclusive Italian restaurant where we had a delicious dinner. Then we made our way to the Boston Symphony Hall, which Una pointed out was among the top three Concert Halls in the world for acoustic quality and it is certainly considered to be the finest in the United States. It made a great impression, even before we entered: I had never seen so many limousines in the same place at the same time. Inside, the hall was set up with small cocktail tables and chairs. We took our table and then, all of a sudden, everything fell quiet and onto the stage walked John Williams, the famous composer of the Star Wars music and many other famous soundtracks. I had already seen him on TV in Ireland, but I had never imagined that I would have the pleasure of seeing him conduct live. The concert was fantastic. Under John Williams' baton, the orchestra played so many of my favourites from musicals such as "The Sound of Music" and "South Pacific". At the end, we all sang out the Woodie Guthrie anthem, "This Land is Your Land", and everyone kept on clapping in a standing ovation that seemed to go on forever. Nobody wanted that wonderful concert to end.

While our mother rested one morning, Una took me to a recreation centre with a swimming pool where we did about one dozen laps. I was glad of the exercise and, on the way out, we were so busy talking we didn't notice Boston Police Commissioner Mickey Roche approaching us. Hearing our accents, he knew we were from Ireland and he immediately struck up a conversation. Then he invited us to visit him at his office. When we told our mother, I don't think she believed us. Next day, however, we made our way downtown to his office. What an experience! I began to think all Boston cops must be Irish with names like Kelly, O'Reilly and O'Rourke. They were all so keen to find out where in Ireland we were from and most of them had relatives back home. I also found out that I shared a family name with Commissioner Roche's assistant, Maeve O'Brien! Over a cup of tea, the Commissioner told us his great-grandfather had emigrated from Galway. Una then told him that I was an amputee and just the previous year I had won three gold medals for swimming. Hearing this, Commissioner Roche swore me in as an "honorary member" of the Boston Police and handed me a commemorative police shield. He told me I was the first person from Ireland to receive this award, so I felt really honoured as we had several souvenir photographs taken with him.

Una's graduation was the following morning, so we had to have an early night. By the time Mother and I arose next day, Una had already been to the hairdresser's. I could see that she was beginning to get excited, although she normally was someone who showed little emotion. It was an exciting and emotional day for us all as we clapped and cheered during the Boston University graduation ceremony, as the graduates made their way up to the stage one by one to receive their certificates. Una looked very smart in her bright red gown and mortarboard as she held up her certificate and we were so proud of her. Afterwards, Mother and I were introduced to some of her classmates and a party was laid on back at the house where we sang and danced into the wee small hours.

The excitement continued in Boston for the rest of our holiday. One beautiful sunny afternoon, Una drove us out to the Kennedy Compound in Hyannis Port, Cape Cod. We walked along the beautiful beach of golden sand, admiring the large white clapboard houses with their rolling lawns. Back in the car, Una thought she might drive closer to have a better view of these fine houses. Finding an open gate, she reversed into a large back garden. Even if I didn't know instinctively that we shouldn't be there, there were signs everywhere saying, "Private". Sure enough, we were in Rose Kennedy's back garden! 'For goodness sake, Una, get us out of here, before we're caught by security guards,' Mother called out.

'Don't worry, Mum, we can always say we're lost,' replied Una. On the way home, we had a good laugh about the day we called to see the matriarch of all the Kennedys.

I quickly realised that Boston is a city in which I could spend a lot of time just wandering around the winding cobblestone streets with their small shops and the older colonial buildings. A favourite place of mine was Quincy Market, which had different kinds of food from all over the world. One day, we had our lunch under the Central Dome, giving me a chance to rest my limbs in wonderful surroundings. Later that day, we sat outside on a wooden bench enjoying ice cream while taking in all the hustle and bustle. I was glad of the rest, of course, because the cobblestones were really tough for me to walk on.

The rest didn't last long because, for the short time we had left, Una was trying to squeeze in as much sightseeing as she could. We were shown around the exclusive Copley Plaza Hotel where we saw the most resplendent chandeliers in the lobby. The carpet was so thick and luxurious underfoot that I found it difficult to keep my balance. Our next stop was the Hyatt Regency Hotel, where we rode in a glass elevator from the lobby to the top-floor revolving restaurant. While Una and I knew it was a revolving restaurant, our mother didn't at first. After a while, she realised that our view of Boston kept changing and exclaimed aloud, 'We're in one of those turnaround restaurants.' From our vantage, we had a marvellous view of all the lights of the city reflecting in the Charles River.

As our holiday was coming to an end, a long-standing friend, Trudy, gave Una the loan of her Chevrolet car to allow us a last tour of Boston. Mother and I felt very grand sitting in the comfort of this luxurious motor. Until then, we had only seen the affluent parts of the city, so Una decided to let us see rundown areas and the sections of the city occupied by different nationalities. It was a wonderful insight into the city of Boston to end our holiday but we knew we were beginning to feel the effects of our very busy schedule as we made our way back to Logan Airport for our return flight. We felt we had seen and tasted it all. Now we were looking forward to having a few hours sleep on the plane. As we drifted off, we really appreciated Una taking the time to drive us about and make our visit so memorable; but I suppose that's what sisters are for. I couldn't help thinking back to the first holiday adventure we shared as sisters all those years ago in Bundoran when she was agog at all the things I was able to show her!

I have always loved to travel, but John is definitely a "home bird". That is because he has always been very nervous when flying. In 1993 I had to coax him into agreeing to go on a holiday to Portugal. Just as well he agreed in the end, because I had already made the provisional bookings! Once we got there, however John was fine until the homeward flight. He loved wandering around the Algarve village of Praia da Rocha, while I found it very difficult because of the cobbled streets on which I always have difficulty maintaining balance on my artificial limbs.

What I enjoy most when away is swimming. In Portugal that time, after my failure at going for a walk, we secured the only remaining poolside deckchairs. I kept myself covered with a beach towel until I removed my limbs. Then I went the short distance on my knees and slipped into the pool. As I swam, John got into conversation with two ladies sitting next to him who were admiring my swimming skills. He told them I had recently won three gold medals for swimming in Stoke Mandeville, North London. I continued to swim for about an hour. Then I hauled myself out of the pool, hobbled back to my deckchair, dried myself off and I then put on my limbs. As I settled down in the sun, I got a few admiring glances but this is something I had become accustomed to since I took the plunge as a swimmer.

Even as a regular swimmer at the Leisure Centre back home in Omagh, I caused an occasional stir. One day coming out to the swimming pool, I noticed that a few children kept staring at me moving along on my knee stumps. As I closed the changing room door, I'm sure they were curious to know what had happened to me. About ten minutes later, I emerged again with my limbs on and fully dressed, and heard one of them say, 'She must have grown legs!' Another day, a few children were diving down to the bottom of the swimming pool, trying to lift a locker key but without success. I dived down and within a few seconds, had retrieved the key and handed it to one of them. I got a few long stares in return. I had already noticed them swimming below the surface of the water, eyeing me up and wondering what parts of me were missing and how I could still swim. I wonder did I satisfy their curiosity.

During our short holiday in Portugal, we spent a memorable day visiting a few wineries, which included tastings, of course. However, after sampling a lot of varieties, it was even more difficult to decide which wine to purchase. As we travelled along between the venues, we marvelled at the wonderful array of vineyards spread over the lush hills. However, a little further along the way, we were comparing how parched and dry the country was in contrast to our own. To crown our day of wine and roses, a wonderful barbecue was laid on featuring all the local food specialities, particularly sardines which we discovered are a lot larger than we are accustomed to finding in tins. Large earthenware jugs full of wine were placed on each table and we helped ourselves to these, now beyond caring what variety or vintage they were as we were then entertained with Portuguese music and dancing. By the end of the night, everyone was quite merry and we all had a wonderful time.

Our final sightseeing tour in Portugal was to a small village with one of the oldest churches in the country. We had to go up several sets of steps to get to it, but the climb was well worth the effort. Inside that little church was decorated from ceiling to floor with biblical paintings and very ornate statues. We lingered there for a while admiring the art and the devotion that had created this special little church and then made our way back to the coach park. We found coaches everywhere by then, and then realised we hadn't bothered to take a note of our own coach's registration number. John and I were beginning to get a bit flustered but, just then, a young woman came to our rescue. 'You're on this bus,' she said, pointing to one of the coaches. 'It's the same one that I'm on.' Her name was Lucy Walker, we became great friends and I always look forward to her visits to us in Ireland.

Chapter 28

Painting for a Prince

After seeing an advertisement for classes in watercolour painting being held in the Omagh Youth Centre, I joined up for the ten weekly sessions in 1993. I had always had a hankering to get back to painting, which I had loved as a girl. Yet it was so long since I had done any painting, I felt like a complete beginner. The teacher was Joan Turner, well known locally as a very fine watercolourist and there were about a dozen of us enrolled on that first day. I had never met Joan before. However, I had heard she was a great teacher, although at times she could be very critical.

At that first Monday, Joan gave us a list of paints and brushes to purchase. Some art materials were hard to come by locally but Joan was very good at helping us out from her own materials. In her house, she always had stocks of items such as brushes, paints and paper. Large sheets of watercolour paper had to be laid flat and Joan always stored hers on the floor under her bed!

I arrived for the next class with all my art stuff in a plastic bag and I was now looking forward to my first taste of painting in watercolour, a medium I had never worked in before. I remember that there was a friendly and relaxed atmosphere in the class as we all settled into our places. Joan began by demonstrating different types of skies calling out the colours to use – ultramarine blue, raw sienna, and light red. She had such confidence in her own painting; she made it look so simple. Yet when we tried to paint the same type of sky, I soon realised that if I were to achieve the high standard Joan had reached, I would have to put in a lot of practice. I think the rest of the class felt the same as we all compared our first attempts. Then as we left the room on that first day, Joan called out to us to, 'practise, practise.'

I began to set aside about thirty minutes every day to paint, especially when the house was quiet with John and our two sons all away at work. Yet in the art room at the weekly class, I still sat at a table in a corner so that Joan couldn't walk behind me, and so she wouldn't see my work until I was satisfied she would approve. So week by week, I practised at home and I sensed that I had begun to improve and really get to grips with water colours. Or so I thought! One day Joan said, 'Mary, you are too heavy-handed with the paint ever to become a watercolourist.' That might have been the end for some pupils, but I said to myself that, one day, I would make Joan Turner change her mind about me. So when I returned home from that day's class, I sat and painted for two hours non-stop! Joan's words had really got to me, but they only made me more determined to succeed. I was so keen to learn as much as I could, that I visited the local library and borrowed all the books on art, learning about the different techniques. I also purchased books and videos to learn from as well. Meanwhile, there was always great camaraderie in the art class and, as the weeks went by, we all improved by different degrees. Sometimes for variety, Joan would set up "still life" projects – a bowl of fruit or a vase of flowers. I preferred to paint landscapes, especially mountain scenes and Irish Bog. I stuck by the principle I had read in one of the art books: *You paint what you like and you like what you paint.*

Then Joan happened to mention my name one day while she was in conversation with Ronnie Kelly, who framed most of our paintings. Ronnie asked, 'Is that Mary who has two limbs off?' Joan was quite taken aback, I was told later, because she had never been made aware of my accident or its consequences. I don't believe it altered her approach to her role as my teacher, but it possibly gave her a greater understanding of just how determined I was to succeed in anything I tried, including watercolour painting. Eventually, when we all became brave enough to display our paintings in the class, we waited anxiously to hear Joan's remarks.

She looked at each entry and remarked, 'This painting is good, but...' We knew when we heard the word "but" that there was something wrong. However, Joan then went on to explain how each of us could improve, using the paintings on view. We all learned so much from her "criticism" and we had a good laugh amongst ourselves about it at the time. I didn't always listen intently to Joan, sometimes doing "my own thing". Yet Joan always encouraged us to develop our own style, so I was certainly following her instructions... even when I wasn't!

After months of practising, I finally became more confident in my painting and I was now capable of producing a better standard of picture. A good friend, Thady Turbitt, suggested that I should enter one of my paintings into the watercolour section of the Arts and Crafts categories for the annual Omagh Show. To my surprise, I took first prize and won best overall in the same section. It was then that I said to myself that I had finally made Joan eat her words.

The following year, Joan took ill and had to be hospitalised. I went to visit and she asked me if I would take over teaching the art class until she returned. I had only been painting for two years at this stage, so I felt quite nervous about taking on this role. However, because I didn't want to let Joan down and have the class disbanded, I agreed. Before the classes commenced, I tried to remember all that I had been taught. I wished then that I had paid more attention in class.

In preparation for the Monday art classes, I usually spent some time on Sunday evenings browsing through art books to find a suitable painting to do. I always liked everyone to paint the same subject and I demonstrated, just the way Joan would have done. Even after several weeks, I was still quite nervous, but I didn't really show it. This certainly kept me on my toes, as I had to memorise all the different colours we used and how to mix them, and I also guided the pupils through the painting. As the weeks went by, I became more confident, and the class members seemed to like my style of teaching. As a precaution, however, before going to the class I always asked my husband John, who by now had become my best critic, 'What do you think of the painting?' The expression on his face told me all that I needed to know!

About this time, local artists had been asked by the Omagh District Council to submit paintings, which would then be displayed in L'Hay Les Roses, a town in France that is twinned with Omagh. A total of twenty paintings were exhibited in France, and I was delighted to hear that one of my paintings had been bought there. This gave me great encouragement to carry on with my art.

Meanwhile, members of the class took turns to visit Joan, both in the hospital and then when she was recuperating at home. During one of my visits, I was delighted to hear her say, 'I think I'm well enough to return to the class.' I resumed my role as a pupil and then one day we were informed that an important visitor was to visit our class in the very near future. I was certainly glad that Joan had returned for that. She then asked me if I would work in acrylics instead of watercolours on that day to show the variety of work painted in the class. I set up my easel and arranged a palette of acrylics, a medium that I wasn't really very familiar with. I was working on a Scottish mountain scene from a photograph, while all around us the security was very strict. We had guessed by now that our visitor would be someone very important, although we had been given no name or other details. Even so, we all got quite a surprise when Prince Charles walked through the door. I can still see the look on Joan's face! He began looking at our paintings individually, talking to each member of the class. Soon he had made his way round to me. I think he must have been attracted by the Scottish scene because he stood behind me for quite a while – admiring my "brush strokes". I gave a sigh of relief when he moved on and was so glad he hadn't ask me any questions about acrylics. There was a great buzz throughout the room after he left, and it took us quite a while to settle down.

I always wanted to try out new ideas in art and so I experimented with different media and styles. Then my teacher Joan Turner loaned me her set of pastels to take home and use. Within a short while, I knew that I had found my medium. I just loved the vibrant colours, how easy they were to blend and that there was no waiting until they dried. I then moved into mixed media, putting pastels on top of watercolour and experimenting with different papers. I wanted to learn more about pastels, but there was nobody working in them locally that I knew. Then I found the Pastel Society of Ireland, formed in 1988 and based in the Belfast-Lisburn area. I went along to a workshop given by one of its founder members, Sam Mateer. I was enthralled by Sam's enthusiasm for pastels, which he described as 'the purest form of painting.' The pastel crayons, he explained, are made from pure pigments with virtually no additives. They have no oils, glycerol, drying agents, extenders or adulterations that could alter or change and thereby chemically affect the permanence of the painting. I came away that day with a lot more knowledge of pastels, and keener than ever to paint in this medium.

At the start of the next art term for our art classes in Omagh,

Joan's health had deteriorated again so, once more, she asked me to teach. By now, the numbers in the class had grown to between sixteen and eighteen members. We also received a grant from Omagh District Council that enabled us to move to larger premises in the Dún Uladh Centre, owned and operated by Comhaltas Ceoltóirí Éireann and situated just outside Omagh on the Carrickmore Road. The facilities at Dún Uladh were excellent – a large heated room, natural light with facilities for having a cup of tea. This time, I had more experience of teaching under my belt, so I had no qualms about taking the class. I even introduced some members to pastel and mixed media painting. Then as we neared the end of term, I suggested, 'What about putting on an exhibition of all our work?'

The reply was very positive: 'Why not?' So we agreed how many paintings each member would exhibit and we decided to call the exhibition, "Painting for Pleasure". It was aptly named! I then booked the gallery space above the Tourist Information Centre in the centre of Omagh and filled in the necessary forms for our exhibition there. There was an air of excitement and anticipation in the class as the exhibition date drew near. We made out a list of guests that we wanted to invite to the launch and this was then given to the local council administration, which agreed to send out the invitations.

I remember saying to the class, 'Invite all your friends and family and don't leave anyone out.' It was a bit like making out a wedding guest list for as many as possible.

We also agreed that, if possible, each individual member would be responsible for handling his or her own work. So on the day of the exhibition, we all arrived early and my husband John came along to give us a hand with the final arrangements. The pictures arrived in all shapes and sizes, carried in plastic bags and boxes. From experience, I found that standing for long periods on my limbs was too tiring, so I remained seated in the middle of the art gallery and advised everyone on where to hang their paintings. Thady Turbett helped with the top row because he was the tallest and Willie McCarter helped out also in hanging work for other class members. Then Denise Tierney arrived with a tin of polish and a duster to give the frames a good shine. As the fresh smell wafted throughout, a really great atmosphere was building up in the gallery. Eventually, when we had all the sixty-five pictures hung, we stood and admired our work. It was only then that we realised how much hard work had been put into our class. There was such a variety of work. I felt so proud of all my pupils. That night, the exhibition was launched by local art dealer Oliver Gormley and lots of photos were taken for the local newspapers. We then watched as a few "red dots" were placed on some of the paintings, indicating that they were sold. I knew then that putting on an exhibition had not only helped to bond the class but it gave some members great self-confidence in their art.

I was accepted, as a full member, into the Pastel Society of Ireland in 1999. This meant that I could now exhibit my work throughout Ireland with the approval of the society in terms of the standard and technique. Also, my paintings could now be viewed online at PastelSocietyofIreland.org, giving me access to a whole new market. The day that my work was assessed for becoming a full member is one I will never forget. I collected my former teacher Joan Turner at her house and we drove to Lisburn. I had been given directions by somebody who didn't know their left from their right! Joan suggested I phone the house of Mr and Mrs Mateer. Eventually I found a kiosk with a working telephone, rang and Mrs Mateer kindly came to our rescue, following us in her car until we arrived at our destination and delivered my paintings to be judged. We were told to collect them in two hours time.

I told Joan I would love a nice cup of tea and a sandwich, so we searched for somewhere to eat. I decided not to drive far in case I got lost again. We found a bar that served "pub grub" but when we put our heads around the door, we were met with cheers from a crowd of boisterous men shouting for their favourite football team. We gave that place a miss but didn't find anywhere else in the locality. Finally, we gave up and bought soft drinks and crisps at a local corner shop and had them in the car. So at the stipulated time, we collected my paintings. When I asked Sam Mateer how soon would I know if I had been successful, he replied, 'You will hear in due course.' Two weeks later, the letter came saying I had been accepted into the Pastel Society of Ireland. I phoned Joan and she was delighted for me. This meant that in the millennium year, I exhibited for the first time in the Pastel Society of Ireland's annual All-Ireland exhibition in Dublin's prestigious Kennedy Art Gallery. Brian Keenan, who had been held hostage in Beirut, officially opened the show and I was thrilled to meet such an interesting man. It was nice also to get acquainted with other artists on the opening night. Since then, I have continued to exhibit every year at a different venue, including Malone House, Belfast, Lisburn Art Centre and also at The Waterfront Hall, Belfast.

Back home in Omagh, my name was becoming well known in the art world and I still taught at the art class every Monday. A local art dealer became interested in my work and sold some of my paintings that were displayed in his gallery. Local people commissioned me to do paintings and I did several of one popular scene at local beauty spot, Sloughan Glen near Drumquin. Because of this growing recognition, I was delighted to receive the Omagh District Council award for "Services to Art". Unfortunately I was unable to attend the awards ceremony but a good friend, Bobby McFarland, accepted it on my behalf. The same year, I won an award from the Plain Speaking Community Arts Group for the best painting in a show entitled "Omagh on the Strule".

Our interest in art brought Willie McCarter and myself together and, over the years, we had built up quite a collection of paintings. So we decided to have a joint exhibition in the gallery above Omagh's Tourist Information Centre. Willie's paintings were mostly seascapes in acrylics while I concentrated on landscapes. We also have distinctive styles that meant we had a good variety of paintings to exhibit. Yet because this was home ground and both our families were attending, we wanted to put on a particularly good show. So on the opening night, we were both a bit anxious. My mother and Aunt Kitty, home on holiday from London, as well as my brothers and sisters were all guests, as were my husband's relatives and friends also. Willie left it to me to say 'a few words.' I may have sounded all right but I felt very nervous. However, Omagh District Council had supplied wine for the launch and this helped to calm my nerves. Musical twins, Peadar and Pearse Devlin, also set the calming tone with some lovely background music. One by one, the "red dots" began to appear on the paintings that were sold. Later, we could relax and bask in the congratulations of family and friends at a little celebration party. Even then, we knew it was such a success that Willie and I were planning another exhibition for the following year at the same venue.

With my professional success as a working artist, I continued to take classes locally. Over time, I was also asked to facilitate workshops in pastels for local art clubs further afield in Ireland. This has given me immense satisfaction on a personal level, because I enjoy both painting and teaching. In the new millennium, I am able to enjoy the best of both worlds.

Chapter 29

A stroke of bad luck

Our lives took an unexpected turn one night in 1994. My husband John went to bed as usual expecting to go to work the following morning. During the night, however, he felt unwell. I called the family doctor because, having worked in the Tyrone and Fermanagh Hospital with stroke victims, I suspected John had all the symptoms of a stroke. Our doctor confirmed this when he came. As a result, John was unable to undertake ordinary tasks, such as turning on the TV, shaving, writing or talking coherently. Although he knew himself what had happened, he was unable to communicate this to me.

It was a very anxious time for both of us. John had to retire from work and I had to accompany him for speech therapy sessions in the Tyrone County Hospital. After each session, John was mentally exhausted. Yet he made steady progress and, when he was well enough, John became a member of the Omagh Stroke Club. I became a volunteer with this excellent scheme run by a handful of male and female volunteers with the help of a stroke scheme coordinator.

When Bobby McFarlane introduced bowling to the Stroke Club and taught the members to play, he even collected John from home and brought him along to take part in the activities. These are very beneficial to stroke victims, because they involve both exercise and mental stimulation. The club was always looking to widen the scope of the activities and identify people who could help. The club coordinator, Marie Kelly knew about my years in Arts and Crafts at the Tyrone and Fermanagh Hospital, so it wasn't long until she had me involved in the routine. I soon realised that strokes affect people in different ways. Some who are paralysed are not affected in their speech, while those who have most speech defects are often quite mobile. The range of activities at the Stroke Club had to cater for all the members and they usually mark their first steps at regaining their confidence.

The Stroke Club bowling team began to take part in competitions with other stroke clubs in places such as Dungannon and Belfast. This created great excitement among the members and supporters. John was now a full team member and he went on to win several trophies. This certainly gave him a great boost. So as the weeks and months went by, I could see huge improvement in his condition. However, to go from being a very active and hardworking person to suddenly losing one's independence is quite a shock to the system. In John's case, I think not being able to drive was the hardest blow for him. I was so very glad that I had learned to drive. However, John also discovered that he was unable to sing after his stroke, but could still play his musical instruments and that continued to bring him a lot of pleasure.

The female members of the club got involved in art and crafts such as knitting, painting, sewing, as well as the table quizzes. I found that some whose speech was impaired could express themselves through singing and this allowed them to communicate. Not being able to communicate can be so frustrating and sure, everyone enjoys a sing-along.

Throughout the year and especially during the summer, the Stroke Club organised day trips to places of interest and often this involved meeting up with the neighbouring Stroke Club from

Fermanagh. At Christmas, the two clubs met for a Christmas dinner. These outings also gave the carers a much-needed break and in the case of married couples, the carer was usually the husband or wife of the stroke victim, who appreciated these few hours respite from the round-the-clock routine. Realising how beneficial the outings were, coordinator Marie Kelly and some of the volunteers decided to venture further. I was involved in arranging the first weekend trip to Edinburgh and a group of twenty-eight Stroke Club members from Omagh and Enniskillen signed up for it.

This was the first holiday of its kind to be undertaken by any of the stroke clubs in Northern Ireland. We realised it was so important for the morale of its members, especially the older ones who could only go away in a group situation with volunteers to help out. Even going through an airport is very challenging for wheelchairs users, so Marie was glad of our help from the start. In Edinburgh we stayed at Trefoil House, a large country guesthouse with beautiful grounds. It was fully accessible for wheelchairs and also provided a coach fitted with a tail-lift for the wheelchair users. So every day, a different outing was organised. We visited Edinburgh Castle and we were in time to hear the gun salute going off at one o'clock. We drove down the Royal Mile where we viewed the wonderful array of shops. After tea each night, we gathered into the recreation room and put on our own entertainment. John played a selection on his accordion and I sang a few popular songs. We all had a good sing-along, with everyone joining in. Kevin McDermott sang a few Jim Reeves numbers and Marie Kelly danced a few jigs to the accompaniment of John's accordion! Others then did their own "party piece" and the craic was great. Then as we began to get tired, one by one we made our way to our sleeping accommodation after another marvellous night.

We were divided into separate sleeping quarters for male and female members of the group. It was a bit like being back in boarding school for me. One night, I had to use the bathroom so, rather than putting on my limbs, I set off for the short distance on my knees. I assumed that everyone was asleep. Next morning however, Ruby Todd who slept in the next bed to me told Marie Kelly that she had seen, 'A wee woman with her head bobbing up and down,' going past her bed. She thought she was dreaming, so she rubbed her eyes but the wee woman was still there. After a while, I suppose, she realised it was me.

Each morning at breakfast, we had to choose our evening meals from a menu. The first time, I remarked to another volunteer Derrick Gillespie, 'I don't see any potato on the menu.'

He replied, 'They don't eat potatoes in Scotland.' Although this was my first visit to Edinburgh, I didn't think that there was much truth in that and, more than ever, I was now looking forward to my evening meal. We set off for that day's outing to the Scotch Whisky Heritage Centre, where very conveniently for our group, we each sat in a seat shaped like a barrel which moved us through the old distillery exhibition. Afterwards we were then taken on a drive to some places on the outskirts of Edinburgh before returning to Trefoil House. Evening came and when we came down to dinner, a large solitary uncooked potato sat on a plate right in front of me!

Derrick Gillespie called out to me, 'You have to cook the potato yourself.' By then, the meal was being served but everyone had a good laugh and this time, the joke was on me.

On the final evening, we had a presentation to Marie Kelly for all her hard work in organising such an enjoyable holiday. Then as we made our way by coach to the air terminal next morning, we talked of how we were all looking forward to next year's holiday. Probably exhausted from the strain of responsibility, Marie had an enigmatic smile as she said, 'We will see.'

Yet the stress wasn't over yet for, on reaching Prestwick airport, we were informed by the pilot that he would allow only two of the three wheelchairs on board. Marie Kelly pointed out to him that we didn't have this problem on the outward journey when all three wheelchairs we taken on board. Along with Derrick Gillespie, she tried to make the pilot change his mind but to no avail. With the help of his wife and some volunteers, one of the stroke victims was helped up the steps onto the plane and lowered into his seat. The wheelchair was placed with the rest of the luggage in the hold.

When my former art teacher Joan Turner became a volunteer with the Stroke Club after we got back together following the summer break, I knew there would not be a dull moment from then on. And when coordinator Marie Kelly then suggested that we all combine our efforts to produce a large picture celebrating the forthcoming millennium, it all seemed to slot into place. Over a cup of tea and a bun with the new stroke members on board, we planned our great work. Joan and I pretended to "fall out" over our different ideas when planning the picture. It was an act, but the stroke victim members weren't too sure what to make of the pair of us. When they caught on, they all enjoyed the craic and we kept it up as volunteers and members pooled their ideas. Eventually, the picture began to take shape. It also proved to be very good group therapy. We used pieces of scrap material and cut bits out of magazines. Then a photograph of our members and volunteers was incorporated into the final collage picture. Everyone was delighted with the finished product, which was presented to the Tyrone County Hospital. It is now displayed there for all to see in the Heart and Stroke Unit (Ward 12). For the rest of that year, meanwhile, Joan and I worked as a team and, under our guidance; the members went on to produce some interesting artwork. This again prompted great discussions and it proved very therapeutic.

As the year progressed, we also discussed another Stroke Club summer holiday and where we might go. When Marie was within earshot, somebody would always say how much we enjoyed our trip to Edinburgh. We knew Marie would rise to the challenge! We were delighted when finally she announced that our one-week holiday destination this year would be Jersey. Both stroke members and volunteers clapped and cheered and I was delighted because John and I had always said we would love to visit the Channel Islands. As one woman said she must buy some new clothes for the trip, I knew that I would have to get repairs carried out on my limbs before the trip.

I had to attend the limb-fitting centre in Belfast quite a few times before our trip to Jersey. First I had to have the well-worn knee straps replaced, and the rubbers on both feet had to be renewed. My fitter was surprised that I had been able to walk at all because the limbs were so badly worn. I was glad he didn't suggest new limbs because I never liked having them replaced and going through the ordeal of being measured then having to attend the centre so many times to try them out even though I hoped I would have a pair of comfortable limbs.

This was the first time that I drove alone to Musgrave Park Hospital in Belfast. Up until then, John had always driven. So it was my first experience of negotiating the M1 motorway from Dungannon to the city, but I knew that this was one journey that I would have to get used to for the future. For the first time, however, I was glad that the limb-fitting centre was now located on Belfast's western outskirts, because this meant I didn't have to drive into the city centre itself. As I drove, I thought back to my childhood when I travelled with my parents to Tyrone House. Back then, it was a full day's journey through towns and villages just to get there and back home.

With my limbs fully repaired, I was ready to do some more travelling. This time, we were flying from St Angelo Airport at Enniskillen, which was very convenient for all, and both the Fermanagh and Omagh Stroke Clubs had joined up again for the holiday. In total, there were thirty-four members and volunteers travelling and we were all very excited, having heard so much about the beautiful island of Jersey. When we arrived at St Helier, we were not disappointed. There were beautiful flower gardens and window-boxes everywhere and we were blessed with glorious weather, which lasted for the entire week we stayed in the magnificent Beau Rivage Hotel which overlooked a beach. Marie Kelly had certainly done her homework and left nothing to chance.

After breakfast every day, we had an organised outing. One of the first places we visited was the open-air zoo, where we saw a large silverback Gorilla lying in the sun. It was the first time that any of us had seen this magnificent beast in the flesh. There was so much to see and do there. We even came upon a flock of pink flamingos. There were paths leading in all directions and Marie kept calling, 'Would you please stay together?' I suppose she was afraid we were less disciplined than the flamingos and that we might just fly off and get lost! We didn't stray and after a snack, we made our way back to the hotel for our evening meal. We were then free to spend the rest of the evening as we pleased.

The weather was so fine that John and I set off with another couple, Kevin and Lily McDermott, for a walk. We came upon a very impressive hotel and entered the lobby where we could hear someone playing the piano. We found some seats in the lounge and decided to stay and listen for a while. The pianist had a large repertoire of tunes and I began to hum along with the ones I knew. It wasn't long until he called me up to sing along with him. I was delighted to oblige. I sang some Country and Western songs by Patsy Cline, and then some Irish ballads including "When Irish Eyes are Smiling", "The Wild Rover" and "The Boys from the County Armagh". It felt strange to sing without John playing there by my side. But the audience seemed to enjoy my singing and I received good applause. It turned into a very memorable evening.

One day in Jersey, it was so warm that most of the group decided to spend part of the day lazing about the hotel and on the nearby beach. John was happy enough to stay indoors reading a newspaper, but I was just longing to swim in the beautiful blue sea. I put on my swimsuit in the hotel room and, armed with sun lotion, towels and deck chairs, a group of us made our way down to the lovely warm sand. Before long, I had taken off my limbs and made for the incoming waves on my knees. A few holidaymakers gave me quite a long look, but I wasn't bothered. Over the years I had become used to stares. And it was more than worth it. The cool water was like a tonic to my warm stumps.

A short while later, another volunteer Rosemary Fox joined me and we swam for ages in the cool, clean blue sea. Meanwhile Ernie, a stroke member of the club who found it difficult to talk, began pointing to the water. His wife Gladys soon realised that, although confined to a wheelchair, Ernie wanted to paddle in the sea. She said, 'Well, if Mary O'Brien can do it, then we can do it too.' With the help of some other volunteers, Ernie was pushed to the water's edge where he sat with his socks and shoes off, and his feet in the cool water. He had made his point and the expression on his face said it all! However, we soon learned that wheelchairs and sand aren't a very good combination. Ernie's chair sank into the watery sand and could barely be moved. A very helpful lifeguard came to the rescue and he put wheelchair, Ernie and Gladys onto his beach buggy and drove them back to our hotel. Ernie had not only proved his point, I also think he had a good laugh to himself over how it turned out!

One of the highlights of our holiday was a visit to an exhibition of the underground hospital built by prisoners of war for the German soldiers who occupied the Channel Islands during the Second World War. At the entrance to the exhibition was a plaque which read:

Under these conditions,
Men of many nations laboured,
To construct the Hospital.
Those who survived,
Will never forget;
Those who did not,
Will never be forgotten.
This exhibition is a reminder
Of the five years of occupation,
And is dedicated to all
Who suffered the hardship
Of that time.

Inside I came upon a photograph of Tania Szabo who, at only seven years old, went to Buckingham Palace to receive the George Cross on behalf of her dead mother, Violette. Tania's father was killed in action in 1942 and never saw his daughter. Her French-speaking mother, who worked for the underground in Occupied France, was then captured and executed in 1945. A film about her, called "Carve Her Name with Pride", is one of my favourite movies and it was really great to witness first hand some of the historical legacy behind the film. Tania, I learned, lived in Jersey for many years after her Royal occasion. As we emerged from this exhibition, Marie said to me, 'Mary, don't overdo it on your limbs. We are doing a lot of walking.' But I was having such a good time I replied:

'Don't worry, I'll be okay.' While the very warm weather could be quite tiring for my limbs, in the back of my mind I was planning to use it as an excuse for another swim in the sea.

Another day, we spent a few hours shopping in St Helier, then went to see the car which actor John Nettles used in the famous TV series "Bergerac". John and most of the other men were engrossed, comparing this classic model to modern cars. Marie had to go back calling out, 'Come on boys, it's time to move on.' So by the end of the week we had done so much sightseeing and touring, we were laughing that we needed another holiday to recover. On our last night, we had our usual singsong and the proprietor of our hotel joined in. We then made a presentation to Marie, appreciating that she had given up a week with her young family to take us on this trip. For us it was engrossing, for her it must have been exhausting. However, I had not realised just how much walking I had done during that week. When I got home, I had to take it easy on the limbs for a few days. John had no sympathy.

'It's your own fault,' he told me. 'You should have taken it easier. Don't forget, you're not getting any younger.' I remained silent. There was no answer to that!

Chapter 30

Full stop for Omagh

Saturday, 15 August 1998 is a date etched in the memory of everybody in Omagh, the day a huge bomb tore the heart out of our town and its people. Looking back, it was a day that should have been filled with all the promise of new beginnings, only a few months on from the Good Friday Agreement that seemed to be the final curtain call of the dreadful conflict we knew as the Troubles. It was the day of the town's Summer Carnival, a day when the town was packed with family groups from outlying districts who had come to buy school uniforms and other supplies that their children would need in two weeks when classes resumed at the local schools. It was also another Saturday when teenagers and other young people would go into the town centre to meet up with their friends. If anything, the tension we had learned to live with for years was noticeably absent from our minds, particularly in a town that had emerged fairly unscathed by the inter-community violence and distrusts that had become a feature of other towns in Northern Ireland.

It was early afternoon and I was standing at the kitchen sink doing the washing-up after lunch. John was already out in the back garden and I could see him moving about doing his gardening chores. Suddenly there was a tremendous bang. I went outside to see what had happened and I saw a large cloud of dust erupt and fill the air over the town, only a few hundred yards from where I was standing. John said, 'It sounds like a bomb.' My heart sank as the fear rose in my stomach. My thoughts were a jumble and for a few minutes, all I could think about was the eerie silence that followed in the wake of the bang. Then the air was filled by the sound of sirens from fire engines, ambulance and police sirens. Soon the thump-thump sounds of helicopters joined them in a great crescendo of noise that filled the silence. It brought me back to reality and the panic of knowing by the cloud and noise where the bomb had exploded and wondering who had been in the vicinity.

I now recall the hours and days after that bomb as a numb interlude in my life and the life of my community. It was punctuated, of course, by frantic efforts to locate family, friends and neighbours. By an almost extraordinary chance, none of our family were in the town on that day. With the phone lines dead throughout the town, however, we had to make direct contact with everyone we could think of who might be there. My brother Kevin came by to check that we were all safe and then drove down to the Clogher Valley to pass this on to my worried mother and check that nobody from there had been in the path of the bomb. Those initial hours brought a steady stream of mixed news, however, about those who were definitely among the fatalities, those still missing and unaccounted for and those struggling for life and limb.

I remember this as a time of whispered condolences, passed from neighbour to neighbour, friend to friend, of hushed conversations about who was to blame and why they had done this dreadful thing to innocent people. We heard of those who had just passed by the spot where the bomb was already in place in a parked car. Their stories were recounted in wonder that they had the good fortune to get out of the area in time. Others, of course, had been shepherded by the police away from the Courthouse that the bombers had named in their warning as the bomb location. They moved down through the town and into the narrower street where the bomb was about to explode.

The names of all the dead emerged and the funerals took place, one after another. I thought of all the victims I knew, Catholic and Protestant friends, acquaintances, neighbours, family members of people I had worked with in the Tyrone and Fermanagh Hospital, all robbed of life by faceless bombers hell-bent on wrecking the fragile peace that was still being hard-won. I thought of the shop assistants from Watterson's drapery shop where my mother loved to search for bargains on our shopping expeditions. The front of the shop, just inside the security tape that closed off the centre of the town, was a mass of floral tributes, bouquets piled on top of each other by those who had survived.

It was so strange to watch all this unfold on our television, beamed from cameras perched on top of big cherry-picker cranes at the other end of the security cordon. It was like seeing it all from another planet. Here was our quiet country town in the glare of the world's media. From less than half-a-mile away, we saw the officials descend on Omagh and move among people whose faces we recognised. We listened to their emphatic promises that they would catch those responsible and bring them to justice. All the while, we realised that Omagh would never be the same again in the wake of this horrific incident which soon became recognised as possibly the single worst atrocity of the Troubles which we had thought were over and done with.

There were 31 lives lost that Saturday afternoon in August, two of them almost full-term unborn twins. Those who were killed left the pain of bereavement for relatives, friends and neighbours; those who were injured and damaged, kept the pain for themselves. For years afterwards, many of my neighbours were unable to be in that part of the town where the bomb exploded. They avoided it and the memories it evoked of that awful day and the lives ruined in a horrible moment of summer madness.

It is hard to think of anything to relieve the horror of that day, other than anticipate that it was the final full-stop for the Troubles and moving people to resolve to make the peace work under the Good Friday Agreement. For on that day, the fatalities and maimed included young and old, male and female, town and country, rich and poor, Catholic and Protestant, Unionist, Loyalists, Nationalist and Republican. Unlike all the other atrocities we endured during all the dark days, nobody could claim that the Omagh bombing was an atrocity committed against their side of the community by the other. United by grief, we turned our backs firmly on all those who threatened the peace. A peace protest against the atrocity was organised. And as the hushed shock and silence broke on the Wednesday after the bomb, when we gathered with thousands of well-wishers who flocked to the town or watched on television, it was a song that did it. "Broken Things" sung so beautifully by Juliet Turner, a young singer from Dromore, released the dam in all our hearts and allowed us to start living our lives again.

So many, however, had their lives turned upside down that day. Yet from even the worst circumstances, good can emerge. One of the injured was a young boy called Alastair Hall who was caught in the blast in Market Street. He was lifted from the rubble into Slevins' Chemist shop and then immediately taken to the nearby Tyrone County Hospital. Once stabilised, he was then transferred to Musgrave Park Hospital where he had to have a leg amputated below the knee. Like all the other injured, Alastair soon slipped back into his own life, but years later I found out that, after finishing his secondary schooling, he went on to study prosthetics and became a limb fitter. I immediately thought that this was one person who could empathise with amputees. He works in England, but any time he is home in Omagh, I call around to his family home to see him. We have a chat about new types of limbs and feet and it is great to have first-hand inside information about the world of artificial limbs.

Chapter 31

Honours in London

A very impressive envelope dropped through the letterbox one morning. It had my name and address engraved in gold lettering. I opened it, drew out an equally important looking invitation bearing a gold crest, all the while wondering if some of my friends were playing a very elaborate practical joke at my expense. Yet when I read the RSVP at the bottom, I realised it was a real invitation from the Lord Mayor and Lady Mayoress of London. They wanted me to attend a luncheon in the presence of Her Majesty the Queen and the Duke of Edinburgh at the Mansion House, London, on Tuesday 2 November 1999. I was invited to be there at 11.40am for 12.50pm.

The event was called "A Celebration of Achievement" and, to this day, I have never discovered who nominated me to attend. I later found out that only three other people from Northern Ireland had been invited – former Olympic pentathlete, Mary Peters OBE, former Archbishop of Armagh, Rev. Dr Robin Eames and Dominic Pinto OBE, then the chief surgeon at the Tyrone County Hospital in Omagh who had treated so many victims of the previous year's bombing atrocity in our town.

I knew from the invitation, however, that this was going to be a unique occasion. I phoned my mother with the news and then other family and friends. My Aunt Kitty in London was so excited when she heard about it. I even persuaded my husband, John, to travel with me, although he still dreaded having to fly there. In London, we stayed with my sister-in-law, Briege, whose house was quite central. That meant I wouldn't have very far to travel to the Mansion House and to give me time to settle down, we arrived in London a few days prior to the big occasion.

On the morning of the event, Aunt Kitty phoned to tell me she had read the very impressive list of guests in one of the morning papers. 'Have a wonderful day,' she wished me. 'You deserve it.' Briege had ordered a taxi but thinking it was running a bit late, she rang again and said that I was having lunch with the Queen and I wanted to be on time! The taxi arrived presently and I was glad to be on my way.

Then the driver turned around and asked, 'Do you know the way to the Mansion House?' It was only when he laughed that I realised that he was joking. On hearing my accent, he knew I was from Northern Ireland and he was keen to know why I was going to the Mansion House. I explained that, despite wearing two artificial limbs, I had led both a rewarding and interesting life. 'I never would have known, you walk so well,' he replied. I then told him briefly about my accident so many years ago on our family farm. I was glad of the conversation with the friendly taxi driver; it helped to pass the time as well as calm my nerves. Eventually we pulled up in front of the very impressive Mansion House and I could see lots of other guests arriving as we disembarked. The television cameras were already in place, but I turned the tables when I spotted ITN newscaster Nicholas Owen. I went over and asked him if he would mind having his photo taken with me. He put his arm around my shoulder while another guest took our photograph.

The next person I recognised was Olympic swimmer Duncan Goodhew MBE, so I went up to him and chatted because he was someone I had wanted to meet. When I told him about my having won three gold medals at the amputee swimming in Stoke Mandeville, he became very interested. We talked for quite a while about our different "swimming strokes". Then, one by one, we made our way into the large hallway where the Lord Mayor, Sir Clive Martin and his Lady Mayoress greeted us, before we were shown upstairs to a champagne reception. There was a great buzz in the room as I mingled with the celebrities among the four hundred invited guests. They included actors, singers, writers, politicians and doctors. However, this prolonged standing put too much pressure on my limbs as always, so I began to look around for somewhere to sit. I eventually found a wide window ledge and gratefully slumped down for a rest. Another lady was already there. 'Standing is hard on the old pins,' she greeted me.

A short while later, we were ushered into the large banquet room where we were handed a table plan to show us where we would be seated. All the tables were laid out in alphabetical order so my name was easy enough to find and, on scanning the list, I realised it comprised of a lot of titled guests – a Baroness, a Sir, a Dame, and a couple of Lords. I was seated at the end between Dr Max Perutz, the Nobel prizewinning molecular biologist and the celebrated television presenter and theatre producer, Dr Jonathan Miller CBE. You could say that I was in very good company. Further up our table were Sir David Frost OBE and six-times Olympian Tessa Sanderson OBE. We chatted amongst ourselves until the Queen and Prince Philip arrived. Then lunch was served.

I found parts of the menu hard to understand since half of it was written in French. At the same time I was starting to feel hungry so I resolved to do my best. It probably helped to put me at ease that, as we emptied our wine glasses, a waitress dutifully filled them up again. Apart from that, it was your normal run-of-the-mill bacon and cabbage dinner. Only kidding, I kept the menu to remind me that it featured foie gras with truffle and port jelly, toasted brioche, buccleuch tournedos, artichoke hearts filled with purée of carrot, béarnaise sauce, olive potatoes, French beans, followed by lemon and chocolate tart, fresh berries and lastly coffee.

Once we'd finished eating, the Master of Ceremonies, Sir Robin Day proposed a few toasts and then gave a speech: 'Today, some remarkable people have been invited to meet together for the first time, and maybe the only time. They all deserve equal acknowledgement. Some have been honoured often, some seldom recognised, but this lunch recognises them all.'

I felt so privileged and honoured to be present in such company on that special day. I seemed to be the only guest to have a camera, so I resolved to make as much use of it as possible. Being in the company of so many celebrities, it was the chance of a lifetime. I even had my photo taken with Sir Bobby Charleton and Sir Nigel Hawthorne. Sir Bobby asked if I would send him on a copy of the photograph. I did and in return he sent me an original Manchester United shirt signed by all the team. I gave the shirt to my grandson, Rory, who still treasures it. I also had a photo taken with Shirley Bassey CBE and Tessa Sanderson, with Lord Richard Attenborough, actress Diana Rigg, Sir Robin Day, TV astronomer Dr Patrick Moore, wartime songstress Dame Vera Lynn OBE, and even our own beloved local surgeon from Omagh, Dominic Pinto OBE. I also got quite a few autographs as we all mingled and talked to each other until parting. Everyone seemed to linger as long as possible; we were having such a good day that nobody wanted to go home.

Then as I emerged from the Mansion House into the cold November air, my brain was trying to absorb the memories of all the wonderful people I had met. Very shortly, Aunt Kitty and John arrived and as we made our way back to Briege's house, they had so many questions:

'Who did you meet?'

'What did the meal consist of?'

'What's the inside of the Mansion House like?'

I was still on "cloud nine" and tried to answer as much as I could remember. At Briege's, I rang my mother who was waiting anxiously to hear about my big day. That night, I was glad to take my limbs off and have a good night's sleep because I had another important appointment the following day.

My rehabilitation consultant at Musgrave Park Hospital in Belfast, Roger Parke, had known about my trip to London so he thought it would be a good opportunity to have a consultation about my left stump with Dr Sooriakumaran, the consultant in Queen Mary's Hospital, Roehampton, London. So in that hospital's Douglas Bader Rehabilitation Centre, I had several X-rays taken and these were examined to find out what type of limb was best suited to me. The findings were then sent to Dr Parke back in Belfast, whereupon I was fitted for a new type of limb to give more support to my left knee. Dr Parke also advised me to experiment with different types of feet that were coming on the market at that time. Prior to this, changing the artificial feet meant getting a whole new limb made. With the latest technology, feet can be attached to the artificial limb and then detached and changed at any time. The eventual outcome of availing of the opportunity for that consultation in London after my wonderful lunch at the Mansion House, is that I am now using artificial feet called "Trias" and I am very happy with them.

The following Millennium year, I was invited to Buckingham Palace where I was to be awarded an MBE for "services to the disabled". I received the initial letter in June, informing me that I was included on the Queen's Birthday Honour List, and the ceremony would be in the palace on Friday 24 November, five months away! Of course, I was both delighted and honoured to receive such marvellous news but I was less than happy with the request to keep it a secret until nearer the time. The only people I told were my own immediate family but, at the time, I felt I wanted to tell the whole world! I suppose I distracted myself from breaking the news with my next thought: I would now have a good excuse to buy a new outfit and a big hat.

My mother was as excited about that aspect as I was, so we searched around lots of various shops, trying on different garments and combinations and eventually I settled on one outfit which I thought would suit this special occasion. When my MBE was finally made public, I received letters of congratulations from lots of different sources, including one from the then First Minister of Northern Ireland who signed it as the Right Honourable David Trimble, MP, MLA. I also received phone calls and cards from people I didn't even know, but I appreciated them all.

Then about one month before the investiture, I received a letter instructing me to arrive at Buckingham Palace between 10am and 10.30am ("no later", it warned), on Friday 24 November 2000. I was permitted to bring along three members of my family to accompany me. We decided it should be strictly a family trip for me and John, with our two sons as well as their partners Denise and Majella, who came along for support although they would not be attending the palace ceremony. Even after the months of anticipation, as we packed for the trip I suddenly found it hard to believe that I was going to Buckingham Palace to meet the Queen.

After a pleasant flight to London Heathrow, we made our way to the hotel for our overnight stay. Had it been summertime, we probably would have stayed a bit longer rather than returning home the following day after the ceremony. The hotel was very busy with so many going to the palace to receive awards. Everyone seemed to be in a good mood and we met up with a few people who were also going to the palace. Like me, they were dying to see inside Buckingham Palace and we talked of the grandeur and the honour of meeting the Queen. Before going to bed, I phoned Aunt Kitty who was even more excited than I was, to tell her we would meet up with her at the hotel after the investiture.

Next morning, I was up very early and dressed in my hat and my new outfit. After breakfast, I had to check that John, Aidan and Sean had their passes with them, otherwise they wouldn't be permitted to enter with me. I also had to ensure I had my letter of acceptance. So wishing us all the best for a good time, Denise and Majella set off to do a bit of shopping in London. By then, my nerves were getting the better of me. The time warning kept looming in my mind: 'You must be in through the Palace gates before 10.30am, otherwise you may not get in!' Yet I was reassured by the fact that we had seen lots of taxis waiting at the front of the hotel. Then we were told that these taxis were already booked. With that news, I was beginning to get more than a little worried. However, Aidan checked and informed us that a taxi was on the way for us. I already had nightmares of the palace gates closing just as our taxi was going up the Mall!

Then I heard one of the porters calling, 'Taxi for O'Brien' and it was music to my ears. We were on our way at last.

'Going to meet the Queen?' the taxi man said as we settled into the cab and I finally gave up a sigh of relief as we passed through the Palace gates. From that point, I could relax and enjoy the rest of the day.

Once inside, we were divided up with John, Aidan and Sean ushered into the State Ballroom with the other guests. They would remain seated there until the Investiture ceremony was over. With the others receiving awards, meanwhile, I was shown to the large palace art gallery where members of the palace staff checked our names. We were given a booklet listing all the names of those being given awards to peruse as we moved along slowly in a sort of procession towards the big double doors opening on to the State Ballroom. Every so often, our names were checked to ensure we maintained our place in this procession. The slow progress meant that I could take time to stand and admire the paintings hanging on the gallery walls, works by Monet, Degas, Constable and many more. There were seats here and there also and I was glad to sit for a few moments to rest my limbs, but the respite was short because we had to keep moving.

At one point, we were then told to gather round and listen carefully. We were then informed that Prince Charles was doing the Investitures instead of the Queen. A member of the Palace staff told us how to approach His Royal Highness and he reminded us carefully that once Prince Charles shook our hands, that was our cue to say goodbye. I could see now that the queue to the large double doors was becoming shorter; it would soon be my turn to step forward. It came with the announcement, 'Mary O'Brien for Services to the Disabled.'

As I made my way over the red carpet, it all seemed surreal. Then I was face to face with Prince Charles and, in the excitement of the moment, I forgot all I was told about not addressing the Prince. He seemed unperturbed by my greeting as he pinned on my MBE. It was a very proud moment in my life. HRH seemed to have been informed that I was from Omagh and he recalled his visit to both the Stroke Club and to our art class during his visit to the town. He then enquired kindly how Omagh people were coping with the aftermath of the bomb, before we went on to a brief discussion about watercolour painting. Eventually, we shook hands and I made my way back to my family.

Out in the Palace Courtyard later, professional photographers took souvenir portraits of the family groups and it was so lovely to have my immediate family there on that special day. As we left Buckingham Palace, Denise and Majella were waiting for us outside the famous gates and we made our way back to the hotel where Aunt Kitty was almost beside herself wanting to know every single detail. She had to wait momentarily because I was now ready for a good stiff drink! We had a celebratory meal together, said our goodbyes to Aunt Kitty and then make our way to Heathrow Airport where I boarded the plane for home as Mary O'Brien MBE.

Chapter 32
Watching the sun go down

As the time for another Stroke Club annual holiday drew near, we decided unanimously to stay in Ireland because airports are difficult for wheelchair users and their helpers. We settled on a few days in Salthill at the beautiful Galway Bay Hotel. So teaming up with the Fermanagh Stroke Club, about thirty-four of us set off for our very luxurious accommodation where we could sit and "watch the sun go down on Galway Bay".

At breakfast on the first morning, we were pleasantly surprised to find that some of the actors from the former RTÉ hit TV soap opera "Glenroe" were also guests in our hotel. We recognised Mick Lally who played Miley and Mary McEvoy who played Biddy in "Glenroe" and several other cast members who were putting on a play in the Town Hall theatre in Galway City. All the actors were so easy to approach and we told them how disappointed we were that "Glenroe" had been discontinued. It was certainly one of my favourite shows. They pointed out that being back "treading the boards" in the live theatre was hard work compared to TV acting. A few of us had photographs taken with them and one evening during our stay, we all travelled into Galway to see the play. It was a wonderful experience to see professional actors on stage.

Our first arranged outing of the holiday was a boat trip around Killary Harbour with the captain giving a running commentary. We learned a lot of history, including how the German U-Boats took shelter there during the Second World War. Since the Irish Free State was neutral, the German guns had to remain silent. Meanwhile, we were amazed at all the different nationalities that were on board our boat and nearly all these other passengers were so busy with their video recorders taking in the beautiful scenery, I wondered did they miss the experience of actually enjoying it at the time.

That evening, as we made our way to the dining room, a few of us were admiring the large fish tank. A member of staff approached and asked, 'Which of the lobsters would you like to have cooked?' Only then did we realise that it was a tank full of lobsters and, as we sat down at our table, we had a good laugh about it.

The hotel itself was so luxurious that just to relax about its facilities was a holiday in itself. There was a good twenty-metre swimming pool so, while John sat in the lounge reading his newspaper, I went for a swim. On another day, we took in Kylemore Abbey where we spent hours in the beautiful gardens. On that occasion, we were blessed with glorious weather and you could see that everyone was enjoying themselves. Then on our homeward journey, we spent a few hours shopping in Galway City. John was always keen to visit a particular traditional music shop not far from the city centre, so we went there and listened to some great Irish music and purchased some tapes to take home. Even so, John was reluctant to leave the shop when it was time to go. Later, we made a "pit stop" in Sligo where we celebrated the eightieth birthday of one of our group, Sean Bennett. He got such a surprise when Marie Kelly walked in with a huge birthday cake and all of us began singing Happy Birthday.

Unfortunately, that was the last of those marvellous Stroke Club holidays. Day trips now take their place. Even so, there were other outings and at the first of the following year's club meetings, Marie Kelly told me that funding had been obtained from the Northern Ireland Arts Council Lottery Fund for a project called "The Big Picture" which was set up to produce an exhibition of member's work. It would involve Stroke Clubs in Antrim, Derry, Fermanagh and Tyrone. Marie then asked me if I would be tutor for both the Omagh and Enniskillen groups for ten weekly sessions with each group session lasting two hours each day. The Omagh Group met on Tuesday morning and the Enniskillen group on Wednesday morning. A joint exhibition would be held at the end of the project for the stroke clubs involved, Marie explained. I knew that this would be quite an interesting project because I would be working with some members who had severe stroke impairments. It was important that all of the members took part in this exhibition, including these stroke victims. I agreed to do it and all my years of experience in the Tyrone and Fermanagh Hospitalsoon kicked in. I knew immediately that, with the help of the wonderful volunteers, we would all enjoy this art project.

After purchasing the necessary art equipment, I drove to Enniskillen. I was already acquainted with most of the group there from our joint holidays, of course, so after a cup of tea and a chat, we began our paintings. I wanted to find out what kind of picture each member wanted to do. One man had his mind firmly made up: 'I would like to do a picture of Enniskillen Castle,' he said. So I outlined a drawing of the castle and he proceeded to paint it. He was so delighted with the finished product, he bought it himself. His wife later told me that it was such a confidence boost for him and he had the picture displayed proudly in their home. Another woman used markers to produce a drawing of animals and a group of other women made a large picture of a flower garden from cuttings out of old magazines. Each project prompted very good group discussion. However, a few of the men in the Fermanagh group were reluctant to have a go.

'I haven't a clue about art,' they told me.

I replied with a laugh, 'I'll soon change that.' Very soon I had them mixing paint and, with sponges, they laid on layers of paint over several weeks to produce a beautiful painting of an autumn scene. I think they were quite surprised with the end result and that picture was displayed in Ward 9 at the Erne Hospital in Enniskillen.

Some of the Stroke Club members had little mobility and were unable to hold a brush in their hands, so I got them to tear up old newspapers into small pieces. We then mixed the paper scraps with glue and made papier-mâché on frames I had been given over the years. Other members discovered a natural flair for art and they needed very little supervision, so I encouraged them to keep at it and practise at home. They soon found that painting was a great hobby and it was encouraging to see how intent they were on producing a "work of art" to put on display. Yet no matter what level of ability the stroke victims showed, art is so therapeutic in itself. As the weeks went by, we could all see the increased confidence in the mental and physical ability of the club members. As the end of the project approached, we held up each individual picture for inspection. We found out then that, among the members, we also had a few "art critics" we hadn't known about!

Having all had such enjoyment while it lasted, we were sad to see the project coming to an end. It had built up a wonderful rapport between the stroke members, the volunteers and me. This was obvious too when all the pictures from the Derry, Fermanagh and Tyrone Groups were exhibited together at the Clinton Peace Centre in Enniskillen. The exhibition that was officially opened by Gerry McHugh, chairman of Fermanagh District Council. The exhibition then went on tour around other art galleries throughout Northern Ireland. It was such a testament of the value of the stroke clubs. John is still a member of the Omagh Stroke Club, which continues to do marvellous work for its members.

Chapter 33

Family trip to Amsterdam

Viewed from the window of a tram, Amsterdam is a bustling colourful city of ornate houses that seem to have more windows than walls, each with a window box crammed with all kinds of flowers. I could understand at last how Vincent Van Gogh painted such vivid pictures. At pedestrian street level, however, Amsterdam is a maze of narrow cobblestoned streets, bridges and walkways and in many places, the surface for walking is well worn and very uneven. Inside those colourful houses and even hotels, meanwhile, access to the various levels is by narrow spiral stairs without banisters or handrail. So even if the trams were jam-packed with passengers and you had to squeeze your way inside, they offered me a welcome respite from the cobblestones and stairs and a chance to sit and enjoy the view.

We were in the atmospheric Dutch city in 2001 for a family holiday organised by Denise, who would soon become our daughter-in-law. Our group of six was made up of her mother and aunt, our son Sean and John and me. Luckily, our hotel was quite central with large rooms, even if the stairs posed a problem for both John and me and the continental breakfast of cold meats and hard-boiled eggs fell short of the men's dreams of a big "Ulster fry". The hotel was also very convenient for boat trips to different sights among the city's attractions.

We took a boat to the Anne Frank house, and had an interesting description of the history of the merchant city and its waterways. It was also explained why the houses were built so close they seemed to lean on each other and with the narrow spiral staircases designed to take up as little space as possible. Larger items such as furniture, we were told are hauled up by hook and tackle through a large window. We admired the beautiful plaster gable-ends and we passed under several very decorative bridges until we arrived at the Anne Frank house. Having read both the book and seen the film about Anne Frank, I was more than a little curious as we entered the large ground-floor warehouse once used for grinding herbs and spices used in sausages. From the second floor, we ascended very steep wooden stairs to the hiding place in the Annex and both John and I had to get help. However, we were determined to see where Anne Frank wrote her day-by-day diaries from 1942 to 1944 while she was in hiding. A large bookcase was placed to hide the entrance to this Annex and when this was moved we could see inside the cramped space. On the walls, there was a family photo of Anne, her parents and sister Margot, as well as pictures of Fred Astaire, Greta Garbo, Ginger Rogers and other film stars. It was incredible that eight people lived here in such close proximity for two years. Even looking inside briefly brought on feelings of claustrophobia. But of course, it was better than the death camps where the family was sent when discovered in August 1944. We looked at the pages of Anne's diaries on display: *We have to whisper and tread lightly during the day, otherwise the people in the warehouse might hear us*, she wrote. These displayed pages, the blackened windows that they dare not peer through, the pencil marks on a wall recording heights for Anne and her sister brought alive the ordeal endured by this child diarist. It also put into perspective the difficulties I had faced in life. As we all made our way back down to the boat, we were in a sombre mood as we discussed the futility of war.

To relieve that mood, we then visited Amsterdam's Red Light district and found it really does glow crimson when darkness falls. Most of the young women were beautiful, and were very scantily dressed. By the time we made our way back to the hotel and its spiral staircases, we had done a lot of walking and standing. However with Denise as our excellent guide, we had seen so much using those wonderful "hop on and off" trams.

Next day, we visited the Van Gogh Museum, which was close to the hotel. Seeing his paintings was the highlight of my trip and I was glad there were so many seats in the galleries where I could sit and admire the pictures for as long as I liked. They were hung in chronological order so visitors could follow his work from the early examples to his strange late canvases. Unfortunately, my favourite painting "Sunflowers" was on display in New York at that time, but I could still enjoy his vibrant use of colour and varied textures in the exhibits on display. I saw that close up, Van Gogh's paintings look like dots and dashes but, stepping back a few feet his depictions of frost on grass, sunlit mountains and other subjects come alive with his creation of atmosphere. However, the self-portrait with his ear cut off was quite scary. Later, we visited the famous Rijksmuseum, which has paintings by the great Dutch Masters, as well as massive silver pieces, lace panels and fine examples of antique Dutch furniture.

Afterwards it was delightful to sit out in the warm sunshine at an outdoor café table sampling smoked eels and Edam cheese with savoury bread. We couldn't help noting the number of cyclists in Amsterdam where special traffic lanes and cycle racks are provided everywhere. None of the cyclists wore protective head-gear as they hurtled along on the old black bicycles, ringing their bell to warn pedestrians to get out of their way. As we made our way on foot, we had to make several quick jumps out of the way to avoid a collision with one of these bicycles. At the time, we were following Denise who wouldn't tell us where we were going. So after a visit to a flower market with bundles of tulips in a vast array of colour display, we arrived finally at a very dark sombre building. It was a medieval torture chamber and it sent a shiver up our spines to think how humans tortured other humans. We finally had time to visit a diamond factory, where we learned about Amsterdam's history of gem cutting. We wondered was Denise giving Sean a hint, but we all found the diamond factory fascinating, not least all the security cameras as trays of expensive rings and necklaces were displayed. After seeing the price tags we declined to make any purchases. However, we did end up with a real gem of a daughter-in-law in Denise who organised that holiday.

Chapter 34

Precious Memories

I always set aside Friday to spend with my mother and, looking back now, those days provided very precious memories. As we made our way over the Murley Mountain on our way to Omagh, she talked about how many visitors she had had through the week. She knew more about current affairs than I did. She also had more money to spend on herself now and hadn't to rely on the "egg money" any more. My mother loved to go round most of the shops in Omagh, and one of her favourites was Wattersons' drapery shop. She was tall and of slim build, so you could say that she was an "off the peg" size. She liked long fully lined skirts, but never wore trousers. I remember on one occasion she purchased a blouse but didn't like the low-cut front. She soon customised it to her liking and with a bow and a bit of lace it was soon turned into a designer blouse.

She was always after a bargain, especially a remnant of fabric. She would say, 'That's a good piece of cloth: it would do to cover a chair, with cushions to match.' Then she would begin to haggle over the piece. It was something that country women of her generation always seemed to do. On several occasions I walked away in embarrassment, leaving her to sort it out with the harassed shop assistant! Later on in the evening, we made our way out to Madeline's in Killyclogher to have dinner. There she showed us all her purchases and we had to agree that she had got some really good value.

My sister Madeline would usually take our mother to Bundoran for a few days and they would stay in the Allingham Arms Hotel. Mammy said that Donegal was the nicest county in Ireland, but I don't know how many more counties she had seen! After breakfast, they would take a walk around the beach promenade, and then on along the walkway around Rougey past Tullan Strand and back into the town to complete the circuit. After dinner in the evening, both she and Madeline would have a go on the slot machines at one of the gaming arcades. My mother also enjoyed the entertainment in the lounge bars at night and she would sing along to all the popular songs. When I was with them, I would be called up for a song. As I stood up, Mammy used to say, 'Sing one of Margo O'Donnell's ballads.' One of her all-time favourites was "Mulroy Bay".

Days with Mammy sometimes involved a little drama. One day I collected my nieces Michelle, Siobhan and Teresa, and then my mother to go out for a drive around the countryside. As we left her house, we were admiring her line of glistening white sheets blowing in the wind. Later, we returned to find that my brother Brian had been out spreading slurry on a nearby field and the line of lovely white sheets had been in the line of fire. In my mother's eyes they were now only fit for the bin. For his part, Brian knew only too well to stay well out of Mother's range for a few days to allow her to cool down.

With Mother's eightieth birthday approaching, the family discussed having a party to celebrate the big event, but she said that she wanted no fuss. However, we knew right well that she enjoyed a bit of a hooley, so we organised a real get-together involving family, friends and neighbours. We had cake, music and great craic. All her ten grandchildren were there and one great grandchild. My mother was wined and dined and she enjoyed every minute of it. A video was made of the occasion and lots of photos were taken.

As the months went by after she turned eighty, however, she became more and more frail and housebound. Members of the family now spent time caring for her at different times. I called up on Monday, Wednesday and Friday afternoons, and Madeline called on Saturdays and Kevin on Sundays. Brian and his wife Margaret were living close by so they also called on her regularly, along with lots of her good neighbours who also called in to see her. One of her faithful visitors was Mena Robinson. She enjoyed some television. I was often told to "keep quiet" when her favourite programme "Countdown" was on. With a pencil at the ready, she tried to beat the clock and often succeeded. Another favourite programme was "A Touch of Frost".

As she sank deeper into old age, Mammy was beyond changing her ways. On one of his visits to her, the doctor advised her to give up smoking as her chest was a bit "wheezy".

Mother retorted, 'I knew plenty of people that smoked and it didn't do them one bit of harm!' For as long as I remember she enjoyed her smokes. On our family visits, we thought that she was following doctor's orders, only to find that she had cigarettes hidden in every room of the house, even in the bathroom! Any time she "took a pull" of the cigarette, she blew the smoke out the window. To keep her occupied, I brought along her favourite magazines – Vogue, Tatler and Woman's Own. She loved to look at the style and she wasn't one to sit twiddling her thumbs, so she passed the time making small religious pictures for each member of the family and they were great treasures to have.

Over time, she needed more care and help with simple things and preparing her meals which tended to be a few simple dishes. Yet she could till throw a surprise. One evening, she decided that she would have a boiled egg and toast instead of her usual soup or fish supper. 'Did you ever boil a duck egg?' she asked.

I had to reply, 'No.'

'Well, only put it on for four minutes; no more, so less.' With these instructions, I stood diligently at the front of the cooker, never taking my eyes off my watch, until the exact time had elapsed. I was relieved when the egg turned out to be just right. My mother was such a marvellous cook that she expected everyone else to be the same. Even to this day, I can't make apple tart as good as her. Also, she would never use a microwave oven saying they weren't healthy.

My mother passed away on 4 June 2002 aged 81. She left a great emptiness in my life and for a long time afterwards, my Fridays were never the same.

Chapter 35

An artist in Paris

In 2007, I was both delighted and honoured to be chosen as one of four artists to exhibit their work in the French municipality of L'Hay les Roses for the tenth anniversary of its twinning with Omagh. Mixed with my delight, however, I was reluctant to leave John for the four days we would be in France from 31 May to 4 June. Since his stroke, John didn't like being left on his own, yet he and both my sons and their wives insisted that I must go because it was the chance of a lifetime. Aidan and Sean volunteered to stay with their dad for the duration of my absence.

So with that encouragement I decided to go and one of the other artists and a member of the Twin Towns committee, Jean Gregory, advised me to give my limbs a rest before the trip as we would be doing a lot of walking. With this in mind, I bought a fold-up walking seat so I could take a rest whenever I got too tired. I also "topped up" the credit on my mobile phone so John could phone me at any time.

When we got to Belfast International Airport, we were told that some of our cases were overweight. That posed a bit of a problem because our paintings had to be carefully wrapped to avoid damage in transit and with the different shapes and sizes we still had to accommodate everything within the luggage we had. So between the four travelling artists – Liam Breen, Kathleen Hinds, Jean Gregory and me – we began a juggling act, switching paintings from one suitcase to another. Eventually we all ended up with luggage on the right side of the maximum weight allowance. This took quite a while, however, with the result that we had to run to our boarding gate.

When we touched down, I was grateful that I was escorted through the huge Charles de Gaulle Airport in a wheelchair. We were then taken by minibus to L'Hay Les Roses, a suburban municipality of Paris, and to our host families who were there to greet us. I was staying with Claire Hadjes, a well-known sculptor, who provided me with a very comfortable little bedsit. Luckily, Claire could communicate with me in English as I am not very fluent in French.

Next morning, Claire took me to the Art Gallery in the Hôtel de Ville (town hall) to meet up with the other exhibiting French artists. We were introduced to Antoine Rios, president of the local Art Circle and one of the organisers of the exhibition, and we hung up our paintings in the exhibition area. It was interesting to see so many different styles and media – watercolour, oil, pastels, and acrylics in these modern and contemporary works. Later on that evening, the exhibition was opened by Mayor Patrick Sevie of L'Hay Les Roses and two representative Omagh district councillors, Allan Rainey and Seamus Shields. At a civic reception afterwards, we were wined and dined and I was delighted to be told that, next morning, we were going to visit the very famous Musée d'Orsay art gallery in Paris.

When I arrived at the Musée d'Orsay with Liam Breen from Dromore County Tyrone, another of our Omagh area artists, I was glad to see that wheelchairs were available to move around this huge three-storey building which was formerly a railway station on the banks of the River Seine. The wonderful gallery is divided into different sections. On one level, we admired works by the great French Impressionist painters Manet, Matisse, Monet, Cezanne and Degas. Then, we moved on to a different level and viewed works by

Gaugin, Van Gogh, Renoir, Sisley, Delacroit, and Millet. It was a feast of some of the finest works of art in the entire world, but we found that art in Paris is not confined to the great galleries. Outside on the pavement along the Rive Gauche (Left Bank), Liam and I enjoyed watching tourists having their portraits painted by very accomplished local artists, before we were taken along to the studio of internationally renowned artist Laurent Dauptain. We also enjoyed one of the highlights of our trip on a boat along the River Seine, passing under a lot of very ornate bridges. I kept thinking of the song, "Under The Bridges Of Paris With Me", as we gazed on the Eiffel Tower behind us, the Louvre to our side as well as a house where Napoleon Bonaparte lived, and then approached Notre Dame Cathedral. I was in Paris in the springtime and surrounded by all the romance I could ever have imagined.

But the day wasn't over yet. Back at our adopted base, I learned that our twin town is called L'Hay Les Roses, simply because there were roses growing everywhere. We were given a tour of a very famous rose garden and, it being June, most of the roses were in full bloom. It was an amazing sight to see the formal rose garden, where the bright red blossoms grew around an ornamental pond. This was then complemented by an oriental garden, which had a collection of roses from the Far East, China, Japan and India. Along the way, we could avail of garden seats to sit and savour the view and take in the lovely fragrance. On our way out, we passed a collection of wild roses, growing naturally in a hedge. Of all that we had seen, these were my favourite.

It wasn't all a bed of roses, as they say, as we emerged from the garden. I knew by the discomfort in one of my limbs that I had a hole in one of my stump socks. Luckily, there were toilets nearby, so I slipped inside and took off my limbs. I normally wear two socks on the right stump, so I took one of these and put it on the left stump in place of the worn stock. I then reattached my artificial limbs and made my way outside, balanced with one good sock on each stump. It worked for now, but once I was back at my bedsit and had a shower and a phone call to John, I was glad to retire for the night.

Next day was Sunday and in France, that is still a day of rest and leisure. So after a late breakfast, Liam Breen's host family in L'Hay Les Roses took us for a drive around Paris. After the previous day's exertions, it was so relaxing to sit in the car and have so little walking to do. By now, my limbs certainly were beginning to feel the strain. On our Sunday outing, we were driven up the Champs Élysées through the Arc de Triomphe and on down for a spectacular view of the Eiffel Tower. After an "al fresco" meal at one of the many street cafés, Liam and I had our photos taken beside the Charles de Gaulle statue. Then on our way back to L'Hay Les Roses, we were shown some of the well-known exclusive Paris shops, including Cartier and Chanel. Even on a visit when we were treated like royalty, we declined the temptation to stop and shop.

Later, Antoine Rios invited the visiting Omagh artists and their host families to his house for a barbecue. We all sat out in the beautiful garden, admiring the fruit trees. Antoine told us that we could help ourselves and it was great to reach up and pick fruit to eat. It was suggested that someone should sing a song on this special occasion, so I began a sing-along with "Que Sera Sera" and "Under the Bridges of Paris With You". Then we had some French songs and a rousing rendition of "La Marseillaise" from our hosts. It was a very enjoyable party and we could have stayed a lot longer in these surroundings but we had to make our way to the final engagement of our trip, a gala evening performance, where the Scór group from Omagh St Enda's GAA club put on a marvellous display of Irish dancing and traditional music, while French performers provided entertainment in their own style. With official representatives from both L'Hay Les Roses and Omagh in attendance, there were other local people, invited guests and the host families sitting at rows of tables in the large Festival Hall. The entertainment continued as we were served a meal of fine French cuisine with plenty of wine. By the end of the evening, everyone was on the floor dancing. The Gala event was finally brought to a close by a fabulous fireworks display.

As we prepared for our departure next day, I was anxious to get home. Since John's stroke, it was the first time we had been separated. However, it wasn't as simple getting back through Charles de Gaulle Airport as it had been on arrival. Naturally we all had to pass through the security screening process. However, when I was ushered through my artificial limbs set off the alarm. I tried to explain to the security guards that I was wearing artificial limbs, but they made me go through a second time, with the same result. Again I tried to explain, but a female airport police officer was called and I was taken into a small room. There I was able to show them proof that I was wearing artificial limbs. Eventually, I was allowed back out to take my place in the queue once more, but as I moved to collect my boarding pass, I was again asked to step to one side. By now, I was feeling very intimidated, confused and helpless. It was then that Danny McSorley, chief executive of Omagh District Council, came back and demanded that I be let through to board the plane with the rest of our visiting party.

I was never told why I was put through this ordeal at Charles de Gaulle Airport and it wasn't until we were well up in the air and on the way home that my composure returned. What the heck, I thought, I've been to Paris and seen the world's greatest art works, all the great sights and I had a lovely time. I would not allow these experiences and memories to be overshadowed by a bunch of airport security "jobworths".

Conclusion
The sum of my blessings

I have passed beyond my three-score years and ten and I am still going strong despite not having a leg of my own to stand on. A few years ago, John and I celebrated our fortieth wedding anniversary and I am blessed with a wonderful family – my husband, two sons and their wives, as well as six granddaughters and a grandson. They have encouraged and supported me in everything I wanted to do.

Life is good. I regularly take my grandchildren swimming. I teach them to knit, to paint and we work together in the garden. I still swim my half-mile every week at Omagh Leisure Centre accompanied by two friends, Kate McLaughlin and Bernadette McFarland. I give art workshops to local groups, and I hope to have an exhibition of my paintings in the near future. I'm still even hoping to paint a masterpiece!

After our trip to Moscow, I remained as chairperson of the Omagh PHAB Club for the next few years. During all that time and since, it has given me such wonderful opportunities for great adventures. It has enriched my life with wonderful friends and brought me along avenues I would never have thought possible. While I'm still enjoying it in the lesser role of Public Relations Officer, I cast my memory back over some of the wonderful experiences of a quarter century in PHAB.

Having loved pantomime since those childhood family treks across the mountain to Omagh Town Hall, I have been with PHAB to several shows in the Royal Opera House, Belfast, including "Oliver", "Snow White" and "Cinderella". We even got backstage to meet the actors. Also in Belfast, we went to the King's Hall for a "Level 42" concert. The following year, we saw Chris de Burgh in the same venue. Over the years since, we have seen 'Phantom of the Opera,' "Miss Saigon", "Riverdance" and "Les Miserables" in the Point Theatre, Dublin. On one occasion, we stayed in Jury's Inn where, after a champagne reception, we enjoyed a cabaret with Sonny Knowles as the guest artist. It was expensive, but worth every penny!

Meanwhile, Róisín McConnell, Kate McLaughlin and I were nominated for awards at "Making a Difference", a special night with an array of stars: Lionel Blair, Honor Blackman, Gloria Hunniford, Brian Kennedy and May McFettridge to name but a few. There was even a special appearance by "Status Quo", one of my favourite groups. During the interval, we learned we were sitting beside Brian Kennedy's mother and we also met the stars from "Ballykissangel", Tina Kellegher and Michael Leonard. All the PHAB groups in Northern Ireland were invited to a Gala Ball in the City Hall, Belfast. It was the first time I had ever worn an evening dress and it felt great. We were wined and dined and we met lots of TV personalities such as Pamela Ballantine, Jim Neely and Julian Simmons. It was a night to remember.

Over the years we have also visited National Trust Houses throughout the Six Counties, and there's hardly a county in Ireland we haven't visited as a group. We have enjoyed many weekends away and one of our first and most memorable was at the Share Centre, County Fermanagh. Although it was very wet and windy, we all took part in the boating activities. A highlight of that trip was a visit to the Hare Krishna community living on an island on Upper Lough Erne.

We came away chanting! When the Tall Ships came to Derry in 2006, about fifteen members went to see them and, for this occasion, I was delighted to have Sarah and Hannah, two of my grandchildren to accompany me. We were taken for voyage under sail up Lough Foyle and it was interesting imagining how the sailors lived in such small quarters on these old vessels.

We've had a few mishaps along the way. Travelling to Kilkenny for a concert weekend, we stopped for a cup of tea and discovered the tail lift wouldn't work on the bus. For the rest of the weekend, we had to physically lift our two wheelchair members on and off the bus. I was glad my husband John came on that trip. Despite that setback, seeing Canadian Country singing star Shania Twain in concert was the highlight of the trip. Indeed, no matter what obstacle we have encountered, we always found a way around it or came across kind people who were willing to help us out. On one occasion in Letterkenny's Mount Errigal Hotel, a member's wheelchair needed a small repair. A member of the hotel staff volunteered to do the job and he returned the wheelchair in fine working order the following morning.

I suppose the best way to explain all my years with the Omagh PHAB Club is the expression, "Been there, done that, bought the T-shirt". Yet I am still looked upon as a role model and I have always tried to prove that anybody with disabilities can still lead a rewarding and independent life. Many of our young members have gone on to further education, obtaining qualifications that have opened up job opportunities and a more independent life for them. We are fortunate in having good loyal members to support each other and because of this, our club enriches all our lives.

So I remain an active member with the Omagh PHAB Club, which has celebrated 25 years of wonderful activity for its disabled and able-bodied members. I'm often called upon as a guest speaker for different functions in places such as Enniskillen, Cookstown and Belfast, as well as in Omagh. I'm also a busy member of the Omagh Access Forum, which deals with disability issues in the local district. I am still involved as a volunteer with the Omagh Stroke Club and I am also involved now with the Gortin Afternoon Club, in that neighbouring village, where I teach craftwork.

Finally, as my mother used to say, 'Your health's your wealth,' and in my case it is so true because I seem to have an abundance of energy. Despite a pair of well-worn stumps and knees, I still put on my limbs in the morning and take them off again at night. Nothing has changed there and never will, but I am happy to believe that my entire life has been exactly as it should be.